Third Edition

The Ethical Process

*An Approach to Disagreements
and Controversial Issues*

Marvin T. Brown

Prentice
Hall

Upper Saddle River, NJ 07458

Library of Congress Cataloging-in-Publication Data

Brown, Marvin T.
   The ethical process : an approach to disagreements and controversial issues /
Marvin T. Brown.—3rd ed.
     p. cm.
   ISBN 0-13-098889-8
    1. Ethics.   2. Decision making—Moral and ethical aspects—Study and teaching.
I. Title.

BJ1012 .B735 2003
170—dc21   2001058085

Editorial/Production Supervision and Interior Design: *Harriet Tellem*
Senior Acquisitions Editor: *Ross Miller*
Editorial Assistant: *Carla Worner*
Prepress and Manufacturing Buyer: *Brian Mackey*
Marketing Manager: *Chris Ruel*
Marketing Assistant: *Scott Rich*
Cover Design: *Bruce Kenselaar*

This book was set in 11/13 Palatino by NK Graphics,
and was printed and bound by RR Donnelley/Harrisonburg.
The cover was printed by Phoenix Color Corp.

© 2003, 1999, 1996 by Marvin T. Brown

 Published by Pearson Education, Inc.
Upper Saddle River, New Jersey 07458

Printed in the United States of America

10 9 8 7 6 5 4 3 2 1

ISBN 0-13-098889-8

PEARSON EDUCATION LTD., *London*
PEARSON EDUCATION AUSTRALIA PTY, LIMITED, *Sydney*
PEARSON EDUCATION SINGAPORE, PTE. LTD.
PEARSON EDUCATION NORTH ASIA LTD., *Hong Kong*
PEARSON EDUCATION CANADA, LTD., *Toronto*
PEARSON EDUCACIÓN DE MEXICO, S.A. DE C.V.
PEARSON EDUCATION--JAPAN, *Tokyo*
PEARSON EDUCATION MALAYSIA, PTE. LTD.
PEARSON EDUCATION, UPPER SADDLE RIVER, *New Jersey*

Contents

About the Workbook

This workbook is designed primarily as a supplementary text for applied ethics courses and other courses that work with controversial issues. It complements other textbooks that provide ethical theories, issues, and cases. But unlike most of these books, it offers a method that helps students to understand and evaluate the underlying reasons for disagreements on different issues.

The workbook will be most useful in classes and seminars where students become engaged in conversations about significant disagreements. They can use the methods presented here to sort out the observations, values, and assumptions of different views and then to critically examine their normative significance. Students will learn to balance understanding and judging, describing and evaluating, inquiring and advocating—the main dynamics of the ethical process.

The workbook continues a long tradition of linking ethics to public deliberation about controversial issues. Ethics here is the work of citizens. By public deliberation I mean a process where people make their knowledge available to each other so it can be openly evaluated and used in making the best decision possible. The "best decision possible" will always be that decision that has access to the most knowledge available and to the right normative standards.

Chapter One describes some of the general characteristics of the ethical process and sets the stage for using it. It assumes that ethics is an activity that begins when people disagree about what should be done. So the chapter gives students a chance to explore the role of disagreement in everyday life and shows them how to use these "disagreeable" experiences as occasions for starting a process of ethical reflection. Chapter Two presents the key resources behind disagreements that increase a group's capacity to decide what should be done. Chapter Three shows how to use the logic of the syllogism, as well as other methods, as ways of uncovering and understanding these resources. (See Appendix One for additional information on the syllogism.) This chapter is arranged so that participants practice the different steps of the process as they learn about them. Chapter Four provides three different ethical approaches to evaluate the materials discussed in Chapter Three. The final chapter lays out a model for applying the whole process to controversial issues by developing "argumentative dialogues."

The "argumentative dialogue" method brings together two current strands in ethical theory, one emphasizing good reasons and the other emphasizing good relationships or care. Some might call this the masculine and feminine sides of ethical reflection (see page 51 for the role of feminist ethics in the normative aspect of the Ethical Process). This method invites people to use the argumentative structures as a way of developing resources for all involved. Appendix Two provides an example of an argumentative dialogue.

One theme woven throughout the text is the availability of multiple resources for making decisions. They include both the different resources that support proposals—observations, value judgments, and assumptions—and the three levels of interpretation—individual, organizational, and social. They also include the various aspects of human conduct—the context, the agents who must decide, the act of deciding, and the purpose of deciding. These elements of human conduct are employed in the "Starting Points" (Chapter One), in the presentation of the three ethical approaches (Chapter Four), and in the Storyboard (Chapter Five). The resources for making decisions and the different aspects of human conduct provide an abundance of explicit and implicit resources for making good decisions.

As you become familiar with the workbook, you will find different ways to use it. Students can develop class presentations, using the argumentative dialogue in Appendix Two as a model. You can also use the worksheets in class discussions of controversial issues, or students may use the argumentative framework to outline an author's arguments.

The method presented here has been used outside the classroom in corporate and public settings, as part of corporate training programs and public employee education. It has been translated into German, Polish, and Spanish. As we become more and more aware of the demands of living in one world, the skills this book provides will become increasingly important.

For more material on the ethical process, consult my book, *Working Ethics: Strategies for Decision Making and Organizational Responsibility* (Regent Press, 2001).

ACKNOWLEDGMENTS

I wish to thank the many students who have contributed to this workbook's development. Many of the changes in this edition are the result of student questions and suggestions. Special thanks to Eugene Muscat and Gates McKibben for their support at the beginning of this project. I am also grateful to Gene Ulansky, Debby Stuart, Georges Enderle, Warren A. French, Toni Wilson, and Mark Brown for helping to improve the workbook in its various editions. Thank you to Joy Benson, University of Illinois at Springfield, for reviewing this edition of the book. I also wish to express my gratitude to Horacio Bolaños and Humberto Peñaloza for introducing the *Ethical Process* to South America. Finally, I wish to dedicate this workbook to my wife, Erdmut, who continues to co-create a context of care and thoughtfulness that makes writing possible.

Marvin T. Brown
Berkeley, California

CHAPTER ONE

Introduction to the Ethical Process

The Ethical Process helps us clarify and evaluate our responses to controversial issues. I consider "controversial issues" the type of issues where people have different views of the right thing to do. Whether to abuse children or not, for example, is not a controversial issue. I assume that everyone agrees child abuse is wrong. Whether child abusers should be given prison terms or extensive counseling might be a controversial issue. In other words, controversial issues are not only conflicts between right and wrong but also conflicts between different views of what is right.

The process presented here does not automatically resolve these kinds of conflicts. It helps us learn more about controversial issues by engaging in dialogue with people who disagree with us and by examining our positions in the light of different ethical theories. In some instances, we will change our minds, or at least consider changing them. In most instances, we will emerge from the process with a better idea of the merits and the limitations of different positions.

Our decisions are as good as the resources we use to make them. Most poor decisions are made, not because decision makers want to make poor decisions, but because they lack important resources. Often this could have been remedied by inviting alternative points of view. By entering into dialogue with others, we give others and ourselves the chance to increase our resources for making decisions.

The Ethical Process, then, is a way of working together to make better decisions and fewer mistakes. It is a learning activity. Its goal is to increase our knowledge, which will increase the likelihood that our decisions will be the right ones.

The Ethical Process is a guide, not a substitute, for thinking. Filling in the blanks on the worksheets is only the beginning of the process, not the end. If the worksheets open up new areas for reflection, increase your conceptual basis for analysis, and allow your conversations with others to move beyond exchanging opinions to exploring what's behind the opinions, then the process has served you well.

1

KEY CHARACTERISTICS
OF THE ETHICAL PROCESS

The process is designed for people who are willing to discuss controversial issues with others. Individuals can use the process alone, however, by considering alternative views.

The process begins with people stating their views of what should be done. In this way the process differs from those decision-making models that begin with gathering information. The advantage of beginning with people taking positions on issues is that it helps everyone understand why people have selected some information which supports their position, and have ignored other information which does not support their position.

The process uses argumentative structures to uncover the observations and values on which people rely when taking positions on issues. Thus, the process uses argument as a method for inquiry rather than as a means of fighting.

The process balances advocacy and inquiry. People begin by advocating their positions on an issue and then turn to inquiring about the reasons that support these positions. This can be a mutual process of exploring the different personal, social, and cultural backgrounds of different positions. The inquiry aso includes looking at how different ethical approaches might interpret the issues. After this period of inquiry, the process returns to advocating positions that are based on what has been learned.

The process includes both descriptive and normative analysis. Descriptive analysis looks at what is and normative analysis looks at what should be. The process enables both types of analysis by first describing the observations, values, and assumptions that support each proposal and then applying different normative criteria to evaluate the strengths of each argument.

The process connects dialogue and argument in such a way that students can develop "argumentative dialogues" by working together to find the best decision possible.

THE PROGRESSION
OF THE ETHICAL PROCESS

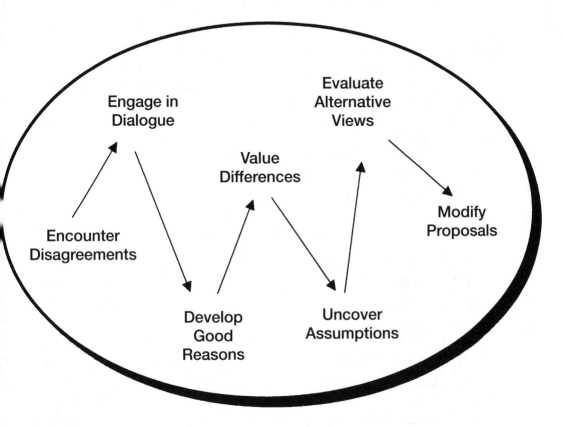

The Ethical Process involves a series of moves or moments that begin with disagreement about what should be done. By engaging in dialogue, members are able to both value differences and develop good reasons for their views. To understand each other's reasons, they uncover the assumptions behind them. With this new understanding, they can work together to evaluate the different views by applying different ethical standards of conduct. The process concludes with participants acknowledging what they have learned from each other by developing "modified proposals." The modified proposals show how the strengths of the different views alter their original positions. In this way, the final decision captures what the group has learned by engaging in the Ethical Process.

ACKNOWLEDGING OUR
EVERYDAY COMPETENCE
FOR ENGAGING IN ETHICAL REFLECTION

Most of us have participated in conversations in which we have developed competencies similar to those used in the Ethical Process. This worksheet offers an opportunity to highlight these conversational capacities. After completing the exercise, you can discuss with others the kind of relationships that facilitate ethical reflection.

In the first column, list seven people with whom you communicate. Include people from different settings. Then, using the scale from 1 (seldom) to 5 (often), evaluate each of the communicative relationships in terms of the seven aspects of the Ethical Process listed below.

My conversational partner and I:

A.	Encounter disagreements	Seldom	1 2 3 4 5	Often
B.	Engage in dialogue	Seldom	1 2 3 4 5	Often
C.	Develop good reasons	Seldom	1 2 3 4 5	Often
D.	Value differences	Seldom	1 2 3 4 5	Often
E.	Uncover assumptions	Seldom	1 2 3 4 5	Often
F.	Evaluate alternative views	Seldom	1 2 3 4 5	Often
G.	Modify original positions	Seldom	1 2 3 4 5	Often

Conversational Partners	A	B	C	D	E	F	G

EXPERIENCES WITH DISAGREEMENT

This workbook presents ethics as a way of responding to controversial issues. Such issues include the "big" issues of the day, as well as the everyday issues that we face in trying to make decisions with others. "Controversial issues" are any issues that arise from disagreement about the right thing to do. A group's pattern of responding to disagreement, therefore, may determine whether ethical reflection is even possible. So the next pages explore our experiences with, and attitudes toward, disagreement.

List three frequent responses to disagreement you have experienced at work, school, or at home.

1. _____

_____

_____

_____

2. _____

_____

_____

_____

3. _____

_____

_____

_____

Discuss with others in small groups the reasons for the different types of responses to disagreement that you have experienced. The reasons may be individual capacity, group patterns and expectations, organizational structures and cultures, and/or social norms. The following pages focus on our perceptions of group patterns and expectations.

FACING DISAGREEMENT

To explore attitudes toward disagreement, ask people whether they agree or disagree with the following statements.

- Most people do what they think is right, considering the world they think they live in.

- If people disagree with me, it's probably because they don't understand me.

- If you are right, then I am wrong.

- We can consider our disagreements only because of our agreements.

- We learn more from people who disagree with us than from people who agree with us.

- If people ignore their disagreements, they will usually become more productive.

- Many mistakes occur because people refuse to listen to other views.

ADVANTAGES AND DISADVANTAGES OF DISAGREEMENT

Although disagreements provide opportunities for learning and for making better decisions, they also entail some risks. Examine this list of the advantages and disadvantages of disagreement.

ADVANTAGES	DISADVANTAGES
Allows us to examine reasons.	May threaten cooperation.
Increases the pool of resources.	Can create a debating game of winners and losers.
Can reveal a proposal's limits.	May delay action.
May prevent mistakes.	May favor "argumentative" types over others.
Can promote a more inclusive and realistic proposal.	May stifle participation.
Creates opportunity for learning.	

If you look closely, you will notice that the advantages column refers more to reasons and decisions, and the disadvantages column more to feelings and relations. To benefit from the advantages and to minimize the disadvantages, people need to make sure that their conversations are supportive of different views and of different ways of expressing them. Sometimes, it will be necessary to examine and perhaps change an organization's culture and structure to enable such conversations. In any case, a group can usually increase its capacity to take advantage of disagreements if it chooses to engage in dialogue rather than debate.

THE DIALOGICAL CHOICE

The first, and perhaps the most important, step in the process of ethical reflection is choosing to engage in dialogue. This choice allows us to become co-learners in a mutual process of exploration. Dialogue involves listening to each other—inquiring, exploring, and reflecting. Choosing dialogue does not mean that we cannot disagree. Quite the contrary. It means that disagreement becomes a resource for discovering more than either of us knew before.

In contrast to a debate, which pits one person against another to see who wins and who loses, dialogue brings people together in a joint endeavor to increase their understanding.

Dialogue	Debate
Is driven by implicit meanings	Is driven by individual interests
Supports strengths	Exploits weaknesses
Strengthens community	Increases alienation
Allows participants to explore positions	Forces participants to protect positions
Allows participants to face each other as partners	Forces participants to face each other as combatants

WORKSHEET #1-1

Learning Through Dialogue

Select a partner and work together in answering the following questions.

1. "How do we differ?" (List three significant experiences that your partner has had that you have not.)

_____

_____

_____

2. "What does your partner know from these experiences that you do not know?" (Ask questions of inquiry to understand more about your partner's knowledge.)

_____

_____

_____

3. Share with the larger group what you have learned that your partner knows that you did not know.

_____

_____

_____

STARTING POINTS

THE SETTING: A group of people must decide what is the best response to a controversial issue. An issue is controversial when people disagree about the right course of action.

THE ACTORS: People whose moral responses to issues are based on their beliefs, feelings, and relationships. As moral beings, their senses of right and wrong are rooted in their social, emotional, and cognitive development. Although they disagree with one another on an issue, they agree to investigate the reasons for their different views by engaging in the Ethical Process.

THE ACTIVITY: A dialogical process that enables participants to work together to discover and then to evaluate the value judgments and assumptions implicit in their proposals.

THE PURPOSE: To increase everyone's resources so that they can make the best decision possible.

CHAPTER TWO

The Resources for the Ethical Process

Q & A SESSION I

Q. You seem to think that engaging in the ethical process will help us make better decisions on controversial issues.

A. That's right.

Q. How will it do that?

A. The Ethical Process will facilitate the discovery of significant resources that are often overlooked.

Q. What resources?

A. There are five resources for making decisions.

Five Resources for Making Decisions

Proposals	*Statements about what should be done*
Observations	*Descriptions of what is, or is possible*
Value judgments	*Beliefs about what is important*
Assumptions	*Taken-for-granted notions of the way things are*
Alternative views	*Other observations, value judgments, and assumptions*

Q.   How can we find these resources?

A.   Through a process of deliberation. Controversy occurs when people disagree. If there is no disagreement, there is no controversy. If there is disagreement, then people must be seeing things from different vantage points. They are interpreting things differently. To enter into deliberation is to explore the sources of such differences; that is, the backgrounds of different positions. When the sources of the disagreement are brought to the surface, they become resources for everyone.

Q.   Will knowing these resources help us make better decisions?

A.   Yes. Always, some resources will be stronger than others, and you can select those that support the best possible decision.

Q.   So, is it fair to say that "ethics" is a process of making good decisions?

A.   Yes. Although some see ethics as a set of already-made decisions—as sets of rules or codes of conduct—these are really the by-products of the Ethical Process.

> **The Quality of Our Decisions Depends on the Quality of Our Resources**

At its core, in other words, ethics is more process than product.

Q.   Most decision-making models begin with collecting data. Why do you begin with people taking positions?

A.   Before we can collect data, we must ask, "What information should we collect?" As a rule, we collect the information that supports our view. If we begin with our different positions, everyone can understand why people select the information they do.

Also, by exploring the connection between a position and the relevant information for that position, we can begin to ferret out the value judgments and assumptions implicit in that connection.

Q.   Are you suggesting that beginning with different positions can bring the other resources into the deliberation?

A.   Yes, our positions rely on them. Ethical Process enables us to discover our value judgments and assumptions and to evaluate them.

THE FIRST FOUR RESOURCES
FOR DECISION MAKING

PROPOSALS

- Prescriptive statements—suggest actions.
- Rely on observations, value judgments, and assumptions.
- Can be evaluated by examining their supporting reasons.

OBSERVATIONS

- Descriptive statements—describe situations.
- Rely on correct presentation of the "facts."
- Usually can be verified through more research.

VALUE JUDGMENTS

- Normative statements—guide actions.
- Rely on assumptions.
- Make the connection between proposal and observation.
- Can be evaluated by different ethical traditions.

ASSUMPTIONS

- Reflective statements—express worldviews and attitudes.
- Rely on culture, religion, and social and personal history.
- Usually taken for granted but may be found in theories.
- Can be evaluated by such criteria as relevance, consistency, and inclusiveness.

SORTING OUT THE DIFFERENT RESOURCES

Identify each of the following statements as a proposal (P), observation (O), value judgment (VJ), or assumption (A).

_____ 1.   We should develop a child care center.

_____ 2.   A growing number of people in the work force have parental responsibilities.

_____ 3.   We have an obligation to consider workers' needs.

_____ 4.   Work and family life strongly affect each other.

_____ 5.   We should be fair.

_____ 6.   Give people an inch, and they will take a mile.

_____ 7.   Some U.S. companies moved to Mexico to avoid environmental regulations.

_____ 8.   We should do what produces the most good and the least harm.

_____ 9.   Discrimination against women and people of color continues to be practiced today.

_____ 10.   All people should have some opportunities for fulfilling their life plans.

Differences Among the Resources

Proposals are answers to questions. Good questions generate good proposals. The best questions are specific and action oriented: "Should we do X?" Proposals are specific "should statements" that answer such questions.

Value judgments can also be asserted as "should statements," or translated into them. But unlike proposals, value judgments are general statements. Compare item 1 on page 14, for example, with items 3, 5, and 10. The latter do not say precisely what should be done but instead offer general guidelines for action.

A statement qualifies as an observation if contrary evidence can disprove it. Item 2, for example, could be refuted by contrary evidence. Item 3, a value judgment, could not.

Some observations include concepts that need defining. Even though definitions are kinds of assumptions, once you have defined a term, you can use it to make observations. If you define freedom as the capacity for self-development, for example, then you could observe that some condition limits your freedom because it limits your capacity for self-development.

Observations sometimes look like assumptions. Both appear to describe. A key difference is that observations are usually specific and are subject to empirical evidence. Note items 2, 7, and 9 on page 14. Assumptions, in contrast, are general. Item 6 is an example. The following chart summarizes the key differences among the four resources.

	Action-Normative Orientation	*Descriptive-Contextual Orientation*
Specific	**Proposals**	**Observations**
General	**Value Judgments**	**Assumptions**

Reflections on Some Tricky Sentences

1. "People work better when they are respected."
    At first glance, this statement could be either a generalization from empirical evidence, and therefore an observation, or an assumption. To find out, one must ask if there is supporting evidence. If there is, then the statement is an observation.

2. "The program is too expensive."
    You cannot observe "too expensive." Clarification about "how" expensive it is might produce a verifiable observation, such as, "If we fund this program, we cannot fund others."

3. "What they are doing is unfair."
    You cannot make a simple observation that an action is unfair. You can, however, agree on a definition of fairness, which will depend on your assumptions. If this definition sets up certain conditions that must be met for an action to be fair, and if an action does not meet these conditions, you can observe that "what they are doing" is unfair, according to your definition.

4. "That's the way I feel about it."
    This is an observation, but it probably will not persuade others who have different feelings. A description of the situation that elicited such feelings might be more persuasive. For example, a person might feel outraged about terrorism. But instead of just expressing these feelings, a person could also describe what produces them, such as the killing of innocent persons. Then others can respond, too.

5. "We should treat others with respect."
    This may look like a proposal. After all, it states what we "should do." But is it? No, this statement is really a value judgment that *guides* what we should do. Proposals refer to specific actions.

6. "I believe in honesty."
    This could be an observation or a value judgment. It depends on its place in the logic of the argument. Could it also be an assumption? Probably not. Still, like other beliefs, it does rely on assumptions.

Guidelines to Help Clarify Resources

- *Look at the verbs.* Proposals and value judgments are "should statements" or statements that can easily be translated into "should statements." Observations and assumptions usually use causal or to-be verbs.

- *Check the evidence.* Contrary evidence will usually change one's observations, but it will seldom change one's assumptions.

- *Remember the difference between descriptive statements and normative statements.* Observations and assumptions are descriptive. Value judgments are normative.

- *Check the level of abstraction.* Proposals are specific; they are things we do. Value judgments are general; they are things that guide whatever we do. Observations are usually specific, although they may be generalizations from research. Assumptions are general.

Some Advantages of Sorting Out the Different Resources

When we are engaged in dialogue with others, and especially when they disagree with us, there are good reasons for sorting out our different observations, value judgments, and assumptions:

- It enables us to discover the source of our disagreement, which may be different observations or different values or different assumptions.

- It allows everyone to focus on the same level of discourse at the same time.

- It helps us listen to one another. The process can be seen as "strategic listening."

- It makes all of a group's resources available to everyone.

- It invites us to value our differences.

HOW THE RESOURCES WORK TOGETHER

PROPOSALS

State what
should be done.

*We should provide
universal health
coverage.*

OBSERVATIONS

Provide relevant
"facts" to support
the proposal.

*(Because) people who
cannot afford coverage
do not receive
adequate care.*

**VALUE
JUDGMENTS**

Connect the
proposal and
observation through
beliefs about how
we should live.

*When we are able to
provide care, we
should provide it
for all.*

ASSUMPTIONS

Express the view
of reality behind
arguments.

*We are all parts of an
interdependent health
care system. Health
care is a necessary
condition for
self-fulfillment.*

**ALTERNATIVE
VIEWS**

Make additional
resources available.

*We should not provide
universal health care,
because . . .*

SOME INFERENCES FROM CHAPTER TWO

The quality of our decisions depends
on the quality of our resources.

No one has all
the good resources.

The increase in resources
usually begins
with disagreement.

When people disagree about what to do, they provide an
occasion for investigating the reasons
for different views.

Such an investigation can uncover strong observations,
value judgments, and assumptions
that will give individuals and groups more
resources than they had before.

The abundance of resources can overcome
a win/lose mentality that disagreement too
easily arouses and can provide opportunities
for learning from others.

Although having more resources does not always mean
the end of disagreement, it does assure
everyone that the decision rests on
a consideration of the
best resources available.

Your Comments and Questions

Write below your comments and questions about the resources for the Ethical Process. Your class or group should take some time to discuss one another's concerns.

_____

_____

_____

_____

_____

_____

_____

_____

_____

_____

_____

_____

_____

_____

_____

_____

_____

_____

CHAPTER THREE

Understanding Alternative Points of View

This chapter presents a step-by-step method for understanding the resources behind different views—resources that were introduced in Chapter Two. It shows how to use the structure of argumentation to inquire about the observations, value judgments, and assumptions that reside behind different proposals. The chapter combines explanations of the different steps and worksheets for each step, so that you can learn about the process by applying it to a particular issue.

Before you begin practicing the process, you need to select a controversial issue or case. Later you will be asked to record your selection in Worksheet #3-1, and then to use the subsequent worksheets to investigate it. A controversial issue is one in which people with different views each think that his or her view is right. So the conflict is not between right and wrong but between different views of what is right. Although the controversy you choose should have significance, it does not need to fit into any narrow definition of an "ethical dilemma." Any serious controversy can benefit from an ethical analysis, especially when the source of the disagreement resides in different values and assumptions.

Remember that even though we use an argumentative strategy here, we do not want to get stuck arguing about who is right and who is wrong. We want to uncover all the available resources so that even if all the participants still disagree with one another, the group will have the advantage of everyone's contribution.

Once we have completed the process of understanding the background of different points of view, we are ready for the next step of evaluating what we have learned. Chapter Four outlines that process and shows how a normative analysis of different views contributes to the goal of making the best decision possible.

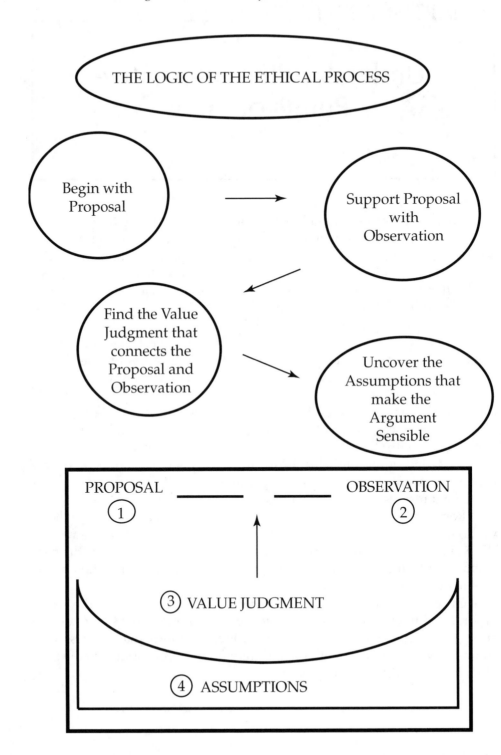

A BACKGROUND NOTE

The philosopher Stephen Toulmin, in his book *The Uses of Argument* (1957), presents a model for understanding arguments that includes five elements. The logic of the Ethical Process is an adaptation of this model.

The first three elements of Toulmin's model are a conclusion and two premises—one premise that provides "data" to support the conclusion and another that establishes a "warrant" for making a connection between the data and the conclusion. This part of his model is patterned after the traditional syllogism, which also contains a conclusion and two premises. In fact, you can use the structure of the traditional syllogism to uncover the implicit value judgments (Toulmin's warrants) that connect observations (data) and proposals (conclusions). The method is presented in Appendix One.

Toulmin's model goes beyond the traditional syllogism by adding a fourth level of discourse—what he calls the "backing" of a warrant. In a sense, the backing justifies the warrant. I have changed the character of the backing somewhat to provide a place for assumptions that express our worldviews.

The fifth element, the qualification, has also been integrated into the Ethical Process as a way to develop the modified proposal. The modified proposal "qualifies" the original proposal by the strengths of the alternative view.

The logic of the Ethical Process also differs from Toulmin's model in that it limits itself to questions of action. It begins with "What should we do?" Therefore, the warrant for connecting the observation and the proposal will always be written as a normative statement, that is, a "should" statement.

Another difference is that the Ethical Process includes both understanding arguments and evaluating them by applying different ethical approaches. The "Background Notes" in Chapter Four very briefly highlight the traditions that inform the application of three different ethical approaches. These approaches provide a way to evaluate the resources that the argumentative logic helps us uncover. After the evaluation is complete, we can then develop a modified proposal that takes into account all that we have learned.

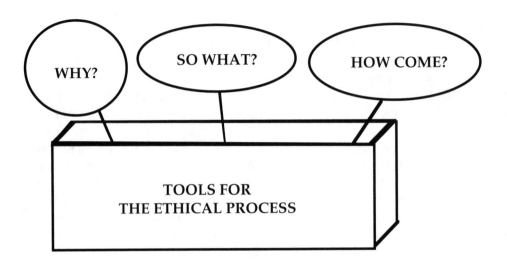

The question **"WHY?"** asks for some evidence (an observation) to support a proposal. Observations describe. Descriptive sentences, however, cannot justify prescriptive statements. What *is* does not tell us what *should be*. The question **"SO WHAT?"** exposes the gap between the proposal and the observation and thereby elicits the implicit value judgment. The question **"HOW COME?"** inquires about the worldview that lies behind an argument and makes it sensible—about our assumptions.

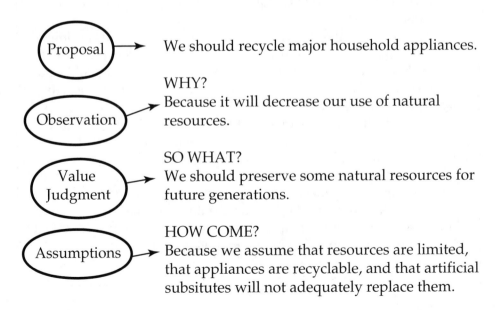

GATHERING RESOURCES

A basic assumption of the Ethical Process is that the quality of our decision depends on the quality of our resources. To ensure that we have adequate resources to address complex issues, we can ask two questions: "Are a variety of opinions represented in the group?" and "Does our interpretation of the issue incorporate the multiple realities we face?"

The first question can be addressed by checking out who has a stake in specific issues. Those who have a stake probably have important knowledge that should be considered in making a decision.

The second question is more complex, but can be addressed by exploring the meaning of issues on three different levels: the individual, organizational, and social. The following chart shows how these three levels of interpretation might perceive individuals, organizations, and society.

	Individual interpretation sees:	Organizational interpretation sees:	Social interpretation sees:
Individuals	Individuals as moral agents with the capacity to choose	Individuals as members of formal groups	Individuals as products of social/cultural systems
Organizations	Organizations as extensions of individuals or as sets of agreements among individuals	Organizations as goal-oriented agents with structured decision-making processes embedded in an organization's culture and history	Organizations as collective agents embedded in society and dependent on social/cultural institutions
Society	Societies as collections of individuals	Societies as sets of patterned interactions among different organizations	Societies as sets of institutions that shape organizational and individual development

Each of the three levels generates different questions concerning the origin of particular issues and appropriate strategies to address those issues. An individual interpretation, in other words, could generate different questions and answers than an organizational or social interpretation. The following questions about the issue of corporate conduct in different cultures illustrate some of these differences. You may use similar questions for developing resources for your issues.

Question: "How should corporations conduct themselves in different cultures?"

Social Level:

1. What are the major global trends and how does our corporation's conduct impact them?
2. Are we contributing to social problems or social solutions?
3. Are there international guidelines to which all companies should adhere?
4. Can institutional forms of discrimination against minorities and women be constrained by our actions?

Organizational Level:

1. Is engaging in this market in line with our mission?
2. Can the people use our products or services?
3. Are the consequences good for all stakeholders?
4. What kind of organization do we want to become?

Individual Level:

1. Am I being true to myself?
2. Does my conduct respect human rights?
3. Am I compromising my values by working here?
4. Is working here my choice?

The questions you ask largely determine the resources you will have at your disposal for understanding and changing current practices on any or all of the three levels. Once you have the appropriate groups represented, then the group needs to decide which level of interpretation should be their point of entry, so to speak, into the multiple realities of everyday life.

WORKSHEET #3-1

Formulating the Question

Describe a controversy that needs attention
at the most appropriate level of interpretation.

_____

_____

_____

_____

Would others describe it differently? If so, how?

_____

_____

_____

Formulate the question
about what should be done as fairly as possible.

_____

_____

_____

After you have formulated the question, turn to Worksheet #3-2, write your Proposal of what should be done and Observation that supports your Proposal. Before you write the Value Judgment, review pages 29 and 30 on how to uncover Value Judgments, as well as Appendix One.

WORKSHEET #3-2

Your View

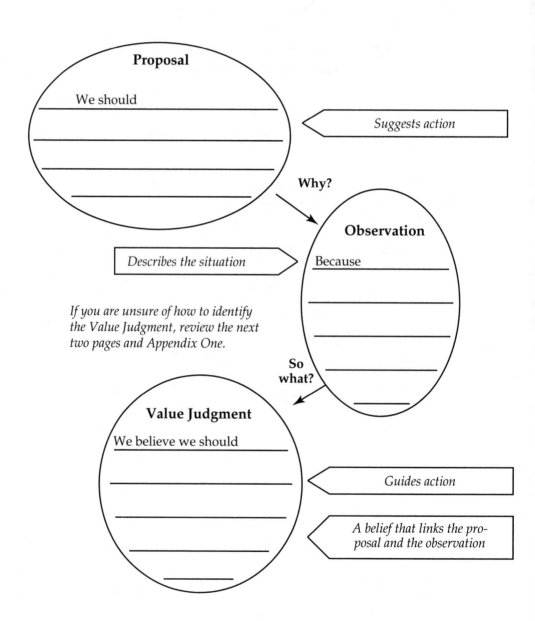

Proposal

We should _____

_____

_____

_____

Suggests action

Why?

Observation

Because _____

_____

_____

_____

Describes the situation

If you are unsure of how to identify the Value Judgment, review the next two pages and Appendix One.

So what?

Value Judgment

We believe we should _____

_____

_____

_____

Guides action

A belief that links the proposal and the observation

HOW TO UNCOVER VALUE JUDGMENTS

The value judgment is what one needs to believe to make a connection between a proposal and an observation. If I say, for example, that the city should install a stoplight at a busy intersection because children cross it on the way to school, you would have to believe that the city should protect children to agree with my argument. If you didn't believe this but believed instead that only parents should be held responsible for their children, you would not provide the connection (the Value Judgment) between my proposal and observation and therefore you would not agree with me. The following methods show how to find the implicit value judgment in an argument. (The logic of these methods is explained in Appendix One.)

1. SELECT THE KEY TERMS OF THE PROPOSAL AND THE OBSERVATION AND DEVELOP A GENERAL "SHOULD" STATEMENT THAT BEGINS WITH THE KEY TERM IN THE OBSERVATION.

   PROPOSAL: We should *reward* everyone on the team,

   OBSERVATION: because the team members *worked together*.

   VALUE JUDGMENT: ALL WHO WORKED TOGETHER
                        SHOULD BE REWARDED.

2. REWRITE THE OBSERVATION AS A GENERAL "SHOULD" OR NORMATIVE STATEMENT.

   PROPOSAL: We should increase our training program
                        for those who work with toxic chemicals,

   OBSERVATION: because it will increase *worker safety*.

   VALUE
   JUDGMENT: WE SHOULD MAINTAIN
                        A SAFE WORKPLACE.

Whether you use the first or second method just described, you can begin your search for the implicit value judgment by identifying the idea that the observation asserts. In each of the following arguments, first circle the idea introduced in the observation and then use it to write the implicit value judgment.

Examples:

We should not exceed the speed limit, because (it is against the law.)

We should not do anything against the law.

We should decrease taxes because (the people want a decrease.)

We should do what the people want.

We should limit the amount of money allowed in political campaigns, because now only the wealthy can run for national office.

We should not allow people to decide when to die, because they may make a mistake.

We should increase everyone's wages because profits have increased.

We should listen to what José has to say because our decision will seriously affect him.

We should share some of our abundance with the hungry, because hunger is painful.

WORKSHEET #3-3

The Alternative View

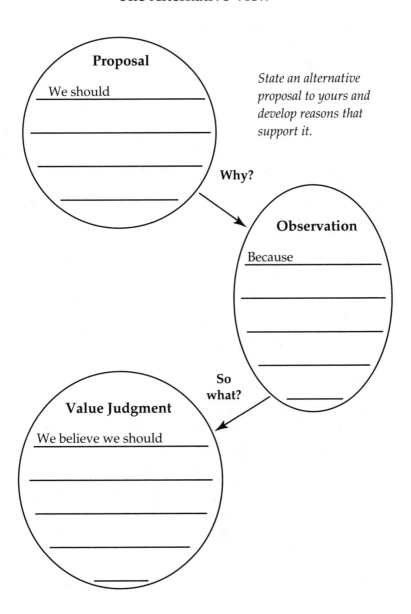

Proposal

We should _____

_____

_____

_____

State an alternative proposal to yours and develop reasons that support it.

Why?

Observation

Because _____

_____

_____

_____

_____

So what?

Value Judgment

We believe we should _____

_____

_____

_____

WORKSHEET #3-4

Reviewing Observations and Value Judgments

Take a step back and examine the observations on Worksheets #3-2 and #3-3.

Are both observations true; that is, can all the participants accept them as true?

_____

If not all the participants can accept them as true, then this may be the source of the disagreement. You can probably resolve the controversy by collecting more data or information.

If all sides can accept the observations as true, it follows that: (1) the source of the disagreement is not at the level of observations but at the level of values or assumptions; (2) the different observations increase the participants' knowledge about the situation.

After reviewing the observations, look at the values expressed as value judgments on Worksheets #3-2 and #3-3.

Do both value judgments express values that all participants could accept as important?

_____

If not all the participants can acknowledge the importance of each other's values, this may be the source of the disagreement. You can use the different ethical approaches in Chapter Four to evaluate the strengths and weaknesses of the different value judgments.

If the participants can acknowledge the importance of each other's values, then the source of the disagreement probably resides at the level of assumptions. At the level of value judgments, as at the level of observations, participants usually discover that they *differ* more than they *disagree*.

After reviewing the Observations and Value Judgments of the different views, work together to explore their Assumptions using the methods presented on the following pages.

UNCOVERING ASSUMPTIONS

If the source of our disagreement does not reside in different observations or value judgments, then "how come" we disagree? Where do our arguments come from? Such questions direct us to examine our notion of the way things are—our assumptions. This section provides three different methods to uncover them.

1. Develop contrasting worldviews and then see whether the arguments fit better with one than another (this page).

2. Imagine the assumptions behind alternative views and use them as mirrors to reflect on one's own (pages 34–37).

3. Imagine a world where you would change your mind, and from this "world" see what kind of world you did imagine (pages 38–39).

1. Develop Contrasting Worldviews

Different fields of inquiry have developed contrasting theories or models of reality. Sometimes we can use such contrasts to identify different assumptions in a disagreement. The following chart of democratic and feudalistic views of social relations illustrates such a contrast. See if your arguments fit more with one worldview than the other. If you disagree with the definitions, use the disagreement to explore your assumptions about social relations.

TWO WORLDVIEWS OF SOCIAL RELATIONS		
Some key differences:	**DEMOCRATIC RELATIONS**	**FEUDALISTIC RELATIONS**
Basis of social relations	Equality	Status
Legitimization	Consent	Tradition
Most important rights	Rights of Citizens	Rights of Owners
Basis for work relationships	Citizen-Citizen	Master-Servant
Employment termination	Due Process	Employment at Will
Basis for distribution	Membership / Merit	Privilege

2. Imagine the Assumptions
Behind Alternative Views

The method of exploring assumptions with contrasting worldviews begins with the worldviews and then turns to the arguments. A second method is to begin with the arguments and work toward understanding the implicit assumptions behind them. The following illustration shows how this works. Carol and Maria disagree about something. Their assumptions are placed behind them to demonstrate that they are taken for granted. They cannot see their own assumptions, but they can see something of each other's. Each can use the other's assumptions as a mirror to reflect on her own.

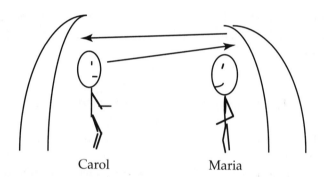

Carol   Maria

Carol could ask herself, "What must I assume to agree with Maria's argument?" (What Carol must assume to agree with Maria, of course, may be different from Maria's actual assumptions.) Once Carol has developed this assumption, she can use it as a mirror to understand her own taken-for-granted assumption. She could ask, "Since I do not agree with Maria, what do I assume?"

Sometimes we can see that our assumptions are about something, such as human nature or social relationships. Then we can expand the model given above to ask three questions:

1. What would I have to assume to agree with an alternative view?

2. What is this assumption about?

3. What do I assume about this?

The following chart provides some common themes that underlie many of our disagreements. Below each theme, contrasting positions have been placed on a continuum.

Some Themes Our Assumptions Are About

HOW WE DISCOVER THE TRUTH

Listen to experts   Engage in dialogue

WHAT NEEDS PROTECTION

Individual rights   Social harmony

HOW PEOPLE WORK BEST

External motivations   Self-motivations

WHAT WORK OFFERS US

Intrinsic meaning   Instrumental meaning
End in itself   Means toward ends

HOW WE COPE

Limited by circumstances   Overcome circumstances

HOW WE DIFFER

All are basically alike   Others are different

HOW WE ACHIEVE BEST RESULTS

Independent of others   Dependent on others

HOW WE MAINTAIN ORDER

Strict enforcement   Intense development
of rules   of community

An Example of
Thematically Exploring Assumptions

Carol   Maria, I heard that Wanda is going to lose her job. What should we tell her if she asks?

Maria   You know she's under a lot of pressure at home, and I don't think we should give people too much stress.

Carol   Good point. But I would have to tell her, because it's the truth and I think we should always tell the truth.

Maria   To agree with you, I would have to assume that we should not take into account a person's particular circumstances. But I assume that a person's circumstances do make a difference.

Carol   I guess I am assuming that the truth will always prevail. To agree with you, I would have to assume that Wanda and I are very different, since I know I would want to be told. You see, I assume that we are all pretty much alike.

Maria   Well, that is a big assumption. I don't know what I would want if I were in Wanda's shoes, but maybe it would be something different from what I would want in my own shoes.

Carol   Can you imagine a world where you would change your mind?

Maria   Yes, a world where spiritual beings always give enough support for every crisis, in that world I would change my mind. In the real world, however, events can overwhelm people.

Carol   Maybe that's where we disagree. I think that people can always rise to the occasion. That's part of the mystery of life. I do know that that is not always true, but it seems like it could be.

Maria   The question is whether it's true in this case. Maybe we can talk with Wanda about how she is doing.

Carol   That sounds like a good idea. I certainly do not want to push Wanda over the edge by giving her more than she can handle right now.

WORKSHEET #3-5

Using Alternative Arguments
to Uncover Your Assumptions

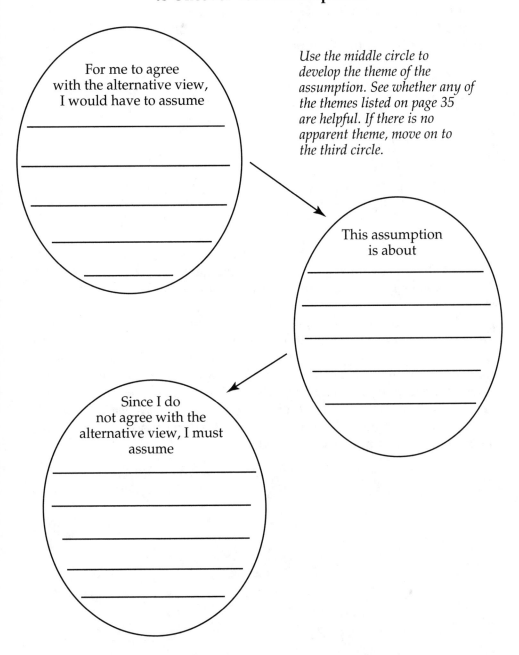

For me to agree
with the alternative view,
I would have to assume

_____

_____

_____

_____

*Use the middle circle to
develop the theme of the
assumption. See whether any of
the themes listed on page 35
are helpful. If there is no
apparent theme, move on to
the third circle.*

This assumption
is about

_____

_____

_____

_____

Since I do
not agree with the
alternative view, I must
assume

_____

_____

_____

_____

3. Imagine a World Where You Would Change Your Mind

A third way to uncover assumptions is to imagine a world where you would change your mind. Like the second method, this one also uses a different world as a mirror to reflect some light on the world we take for granted, that is, on our assumptions.

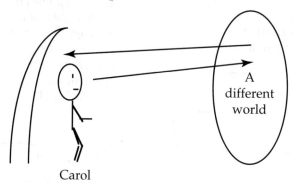

Carol

Carol could say in this case, "If the world were 'such and such,' then I would change my mind." Once she has imagined this world, she can ask herself, "Since I am not assuming such a world, what kind of world am I assuming?"

The goal of these strategies for uncovering assumptions is to learn more about our own assumptions than we knew before. The second and third methods begin by acknowledging that we do not know what assumptions are relevant for this issue. We learn this by stepping into the shoes of another or by imagining a different world. We then use these different assumptions as a way of reflecting on our own. We learn about our assumptions, in other words, from people who differ from us or from situations that we do not take for granted.

WORKSHEET #3-6

Imagining a Different World
to Uncover the World You Assume

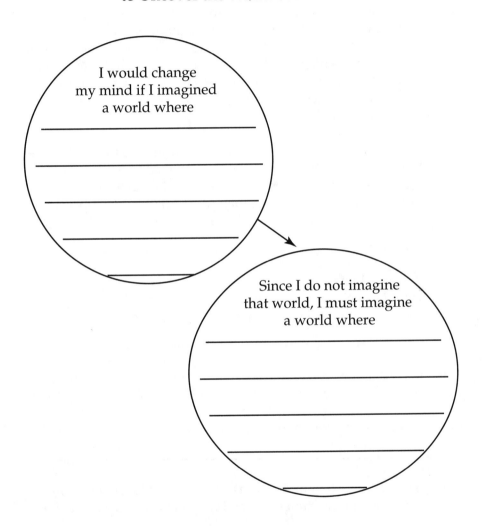

I would change
my mind if I imagined
a world where

_____

_____

_____

_____

Since I do not imagine
that world, I must imagine
a world where

_____

_____

_____

_____

WORKSHEET #3-7

Reviewing Assumptions

Take a step back and examine the assumptions on Worksheets #3-5 and #3-6 (pages 37 and 39). Make sure that the assumptions are not merely re-statements of the observations or value judgments. Assumptions express the worldviews from which you observe and evaluate. If the assumptions are the source of the initial disagreement about what to do, then they probably conflict with each other. The following suggestions may help to determine the nature of the conflict.

- Sometimes the conflict is only apparent, such as the conflict between cooperation and competition. Instead of being opposed to each other, one provides the context for the other—cooperation provides the context for competition. Can you develop a similar contextual relationship between these assumptions?

- If the conflict is between mutually exclusive assumptions, can you place them on a continuum, like the continuums on page 35, and then determine the proper balance between the extremes?

If the conflict between the two assumptions remains, then you can ask whether one assumption has more merit in this case than the other.

- Is one assumption more relevant to the issue?

- Is one assumption more consistent with conduct in other situations and at other times? If not, is the inconsistency justifiable?

- Is one assumption more inclusive? (An assumption that denies significant experiences would not hold up as well as one that includes them.)

AN EXAMPLE OF UNDERSTANDING ALTERNATIVE POINTS OF VIEW

Should Joan leave the university for a better job, or should she stay for six months and help her team finish its project?

Joan should stay.	Joan should leave.
Because the team members have agreed to work together on this project.	Because the new job provides opportunities for her career development.
People should keep their promises.	People should increase their competence and develop their potential.
The alternative view may assume that individuals cannot develop their potential in groups, so I may assume that they can.	The first view may assume that relationships are more essential than individual achievement, so I may assume the opposite.

Joan decides to leave because the team cannot imagine how to change her work to allow her to develop her potential and it appears that the team can finish the work without her.

Q & A SESSION II

Q.   How do you evaluate the quality of the observations, values, and assumptions?

A.   The observations are the easiest to evaluate. You simply examine the strength of the evidence that supports them.

Q.   In the chart on page 15, observations are listed as specific. Can there also be general observations?

A.   Yes. They too would be supported by evidence. For example, a statement like "Children learn faster in a secure environment" would be considered an observation if it was supported by research on child development.

Q.   Doesn't that look like an assumption?

A.   It could be an assumption. It depends on whether the statement relies on evidence. If someone continues to hold it despite evidence to the contrary, then it is an assumption.

Q.   So a general statement may be an assumption even though it was presented as an observation.

A.   Right. It depends on the statement's dependence on evidence.

Q.   This process is somewhat more complicated than it first appears.

A.   True.

Q.   OK. So we can evaluate observations by examining the evidence that supports them. How can we evaluate assumptions?

A.   You can use the criteria of relevance and consistency. You may also know theories, such as theories of human nature, which you can use to analyze assumptions.

Q.   What do you mean by relevance?

A.   Consider the use of stereotypes. A stereotype is a general characteristic. Stereotyping is applying the general characteristic to a particular person or situation. Stereotyping often misleads us because the particular case differs significantly from the general characteristic.

Q.   How can you tell when you are stereotyping?

A. We usually find out only in dialogue with others, when we begin to compare and contrast our assumptions and examine which ones seem more connected to the situation.

Q. OK. Could you say something about the criterion of consistency?

A. Sure. Let's say that we uncover an assumption that posits a radical individuality—the common assumption of the "self-made man." We can ask if this assumption is consistent with anyone's human experience. Did the person give birth to himself, nurture himself, learn by himself, and so on? Obviously not. So the assumption is inconsistent with some basic human experiences.

Q. So what?

A. I can see you are learning how to use this process! Certainly, assumptions that do not contradict basic human experiences are better than those that do. If you continue to engage in the exploration of assumptions, you will probably find yourself seeking consistency among them.

Q. You may be right. But don't you mean consistency among assumptions, not consistency between assumptions and experiences?

A. True. These are two different types of consistency. I think we can use both to evaluate the assumptions that we uncover.

Q. So we evaluate our observations by examining the strength of the evidence that supports them and we evaluate assumptions by the criteria of relevance and consistency. How do we evaluate our value judgments?

A. I'm glad you asked. The next chapter addresses that question.

WORKSHEET #3-8

Developing Alternative Views

Select a disagreement and refer to the previous worksheets to develop your view and an alternative view following the steps from 1 to 8.

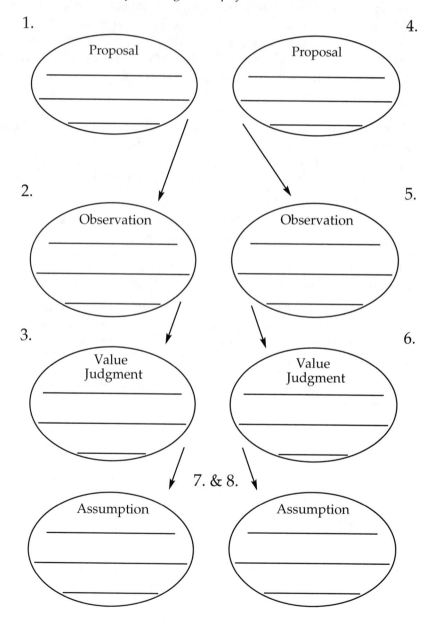

Your Comments and Questions

Write below your comments and questions about discovering different resources—observations, value judgments, and assumptions—by working with alternative views.

_____

_____

_____

_____

_____

_____

_____

_____

_____

_____

_____

_____

_____

_____

_____

_____

CHAPTER FOUR

Evaluating Arguments from Different Ethical Approaches

In Chapter Three, we completed half of the Ethical Process. We learned to access the knowledge behind different proposals—the observations, value judgments, and assumptions. In this chapter, we conclude the process by evaluating the different value judgments and assumptions we have uncovered and then developing a modified proposal about what we should do.

This chapter gives us resources to answer the question, "How do we evaluate different value judgments?" For these resources to be adequate, they must be normative and comprehensive. By normative we mean that they express general standards or norms we can use to evaluate alternative views. By comprehensive we mean that they must cover the whole spectrum of human conduct.

So what normative standards should we use? Can we use just one or do we need more than one? We need enough to cover the essential components of human conduct. And what are these components? The social philosopher Kenneth Burke suggested that to have a comprehensive analysis of human conduct, we need to consider five elements, which he calls a Pentad (*A Grammar of Motives*, 1969). The five are Scene, Agent, Act, Agency, and Purpose.

- Scene: the situation in which an act occurs. It may include past, present, and future times and other persons or groups, as well as the natural environment.

- Agent: whoever has the power to act, the capacity to consider different actions, and the ability to justify the action. This may include organizations as well as persons, since organizations also have to choose among options and justify their choices.

- Act: what an agent decides to do. Ethics sees agents as deciding to act, rather than being "moved" by something. Acts imply decisions.

- Agency: how something is achieved. Terms such as *method, procedure,* and *means* belong to agency. Agency emphasizes things as instruments in a process.

- Purpose: the "good" that agents want to achieve. Individual persons, communities, and organizations can have purposes. Many organizations have formulated their purpose in their "Mission" or "Aspiration" statements.

The three ethical theories presented in this chapter cover all five elements. Each is a complete theory in itself, with its own method for arriving at a right decision. The traditional labels are teleology, deontology, and utilitarianism, but we will call them by their normative criterion for justifying actions: an ethics of purpose, an ethics of principle, and an ethics of consequence.

An ethics of purpose covers agent, purpose, and act. It begins with the agent—an individual, group, or organization—deciding what its "good" purposes are, and then asking what particular action (act) can bring about those purposes. It also may look at acts as an agency; that is, as a means to achieve an end. The purposes include both what the agent should achieve and what it should become, which we will call the external and internal purposes. The following diagram illustrates the method of analysis this approach takes:

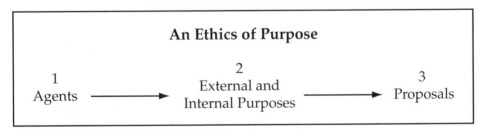

An Ethics of Purpose

| 1 Agents | → | 2 External and Internal Purposes | → | 3 Proposals |

An ethics of principle focuses on the act and the agent. It seeks the implicit principle of an action and then tests its validity by seeing if one can will it as a universal moral law, and if it recognizes the moral agency of others. The normative criterion for an ethics of principle is moral consistency. In some cases, you can also use this scheme to think about social justice and human rights. The implicit principles function as principles of justice and the recognition of moral agency would entail respect of human rights.

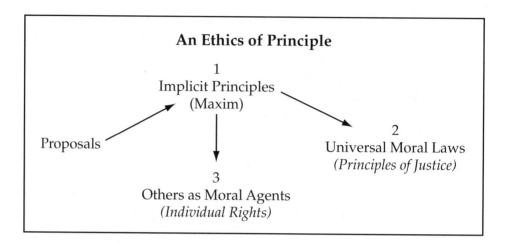

An ethics of consequence covers the area not covered by the other two approaches—the situation. It begins with the result of the act, by looking at what impact it will have on the situation (Burke's Scene). Since its normative criterion is the utilitarian principle of the greatest good for the greatest number, you will have to list the groups affected by an act before you list the consequences.

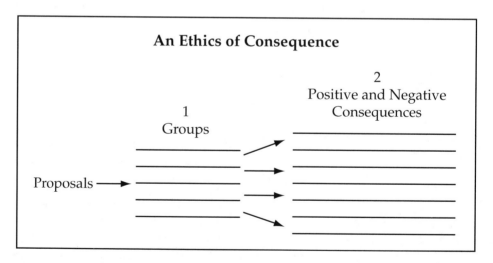

The following chart shows the relationships among the three ethical approaches and the elements of human conduct. The numbers indicate the sequence among the elements for each of the ethical approaches. The chart as a whole demonstrates that the three approaches do cover all five elements.

	FIVE ELEMENTS OF HUMAN CONDUCT				
	SCENE	**AGENT**	**ACT**	**AGENCY**	**PURPOSE**
	When? Where?	**Who?**	**What?**	**How?**	**Why?**
Ethics of Purpose		**1** Who is deciding?	**3.1** Will this Act achieve those purposes?	**3.2** (Is the Act the right means to achieve the end?)	**2** What are the Agent's Purposes?
Ethics of Principle		**2** Does the Act treat others with respect?	**1** Can you will the Act's maxim as a moral law?		
Ethics of Consequence	**1** What groups (environments) are affected?			**2** How will the Act impact these groups?	

These three ethical approaches, of course, are not the only ethical theories that are part of current literature on ethics. Other ethical theories could find their place on this chart. *Virtue ethics*, for example, would fit under an ethics of purpose, with special focus on the character of the agent or internal purpose. *An ethics of responsibility* would belong to an ethics of consequence as it directs our attention toward being responsive to the possible impact of our actions. *An ethics of care* or feministic ethic can also be embedded in the three ethical approaches. An ethics of care actually expands our understanding of these approaches, which we will consider on page 52.

BACKGROUND NOTES ON THE THREE ETHICAL APPROACHES

An ethics of purpose has its roots in Aristotle's philosophy. His *Nicomachean Ethics* begins, "Every art and every investigation, and likewise every practical pursuit or undertaking, seems to aim at some good: hence it has been well said that the Good is That at which all things aim." For Aristotle, our highest purpose or "telos" is happiness, which he understands as a full flourishing of the self. This includes both *doing* something well and *being* a good person. In Aristotle we find an emphasis both on decision making and on the virtues or dispositions that help us know what to decide. In recent times, this approach can be seen as embedded in such notions as an individual developing his or her best potential, an organization's mission or function in society, and a people's vision of its future.

An ethics of principle stems from the philosophy of Immanuel Kant. Writing in late-eighteenth-century Germany, Kant sought an ethic that preserves human freedom by giving people a way of discerning their obligations. Assuming that we want to do the right thing, he believed we can judge an act by considering whether we could will that the act's implicit principle become a universal moral law. Such a moral law would be one that could be consistently held in all similar situations. Since human beings freely decide their obligations, they deserve to be respected. In recent thinking, an ethics of principle approach has found expression in discussions of human rights and social justice, especially when these are seen as ways of preserving human freedom.

An ethics of consequence comes from the work of Jeremy Betham, usually recognized as the father of utilitarianism, and John Stuart Mill. Writing in eighteenth-century England when traditional authorities were losing their legitimacy, Bentham wanted to give parliamentary governments a way to figure out by themselves what was the right thing to do.

He developed what he called a "moral calculus," which consists of measuring the probable pain and pleasure of different courses of action and then selecting the one that, overall, causes the most pleasure. John Stuart Mill, a follower of Bentham, further developed utilitarianism by moving beyond Bentham's emphasis on pleasure and pain to an emphasis on quality of life. Mill continued to use the utilitarian principle of "the greatest happiness for the greatest number" as the criterion for deciding which action is right.

Recent practices in the tradition of utilitarianism include cost-benefit analysis, the satisfying of people's different preferences, and even the everyday habit of listing the pros and cons of doing something to help decide whether to do it. Today this type of "moral calculus" is used for individual decisions, but when the tradition began, the "greatest number" was never limited to only the decision maker.

In some recent ethical textbooks, the ethics of purpose or teleology and an ethics of consequence or utilitarianism have been combined into one ethical approach, which is then contrasted with an ethics of principle. This overlooks essential historical differences among the three approaches and leaves us with fewer resources for conducting a strong normative evaluation of different viewpoints. Utilitarianism does not develop a vision of the "good" purpose that it attempts to reach. And teleology does not consider everyone affected by a decision. Furthermore, these two approaches have their way of thinking: An ethics of purpose thinks in terms of what belongs to what (Do these means belong to these ends?). An ethics of consequence thinks in terms of comparison and contrast (Will the consequences of this act bring about an overall greater good for all affected than will the consequences of the alternatives?).

The background and the current thinking about each of these ethical approaches, of course, is much broader and richer than has been presented in these notes. You will need to use other sources to fully understand their possibilities and limitations.

THE ETHICS OF CARE
AND THE THREE ETHICAL APPROACHES

Aristotle, Kant, Bentham, and Mill, of course, are not the only major figures in the history of ethics. The justification for using their ideas is not that they are without equals, but rather that their ideas taken together cover all five aspects of human conduct as outlined by Kenneth Burke. Still, their interpretation of human conduct has its limitations, as has been demonstrated by recent developments in feminist ethics or an ethics of care.

In her book, *In a Different Voice* (1982), Carol Gillian showed us that we need to look at our implicit "images of relationships." Do we think of "agents," for example, as individual, isolated persons making decisions based on their self-interest, or do we think of agents as persons embedded in relationships making decisions based on the relational claims and responsibilities? Another feminist author, Virginia Held, argues that instead of the image of "economic man" as the symbol of humanity, we should use the image of mother and child—a relational image of care (*Feminist Morality*, 1993). These challenges to traditional ethics can help us explore our assumptions about being connected with, and disconnected from, each other. I think feminist ethics has taught us that the relationships in which we live largely determine who we are and what we see as appropriate action.

Although an ethics of care does not expose any new aspect of human conduct not already covered by the three ethical approaches, it does give us a richer account of each approach. In terms of an ethics of purpose, it not only presents the agent as a relational being, but also invites us to examine an organization's internal purpose in terms of human relations. We could speak here of "caring organizations." When we examine an ethics of principle through the lens of care, we see that the notion of "respect" can be expanded to include "mutual respect," not simply respect for the individual. And finally, an ethics of care draws attention to a decision's impact on the relationships in which we live. So, even though the three ethical approaches completely cover the five elements of human conduct, an ethics of care can improve our application of them to concrete situations.

ETHICAL APPROACHES, ORGANIZATIONAL RESOURCES, AND KEY VIRTUES

When applying the three ethical approaches to disagreements that occur in organizational settings, there may be organizational resources that make the application easier. The chart below shows some resources that correspond to each of the three approaches and offers a "key virtue" that could be used in linking the ethical approach with the organizational resource.

ETHICAL APPROACH	ORGANIZATIONAL RESOURCES	KEY VIRTUE
Purpose	Mission Statement	Integrity
Principle	Code of Ethics	Fairness
Consequence	Stakeholders	Responsibility

Integrity: Do the proposals align themselves with the purpose of the organization? Is there a relationship of integrity between the proposed act and the character of the organization?

Fairness: Is this a case of "special pleading," where we would not want others to do the same thing in similar situations? Are we being consistent in our treatment of others?

Responsibility: What groups will be affected by this decision? Do the proposals demonstrate a responsible use of resources and power in regard to all these groups?

APPLYING THE THREE ETHICAL APPROACHES TO ALTERNATIVE ARGUMENTS

As you apply the three ethical approaches to the different arguments you have developed in Chapter Three, you will discover that each argument will correspond with one of the ethical approaches more than the other two. You can discover which one by examining the argument's value judgment.

> Value judgments that rely on an agent's identity, such as "Nurses should relieve suffering," may match an ethics of purpose.

> Value judgments that speak of justice or respecting individual rights, such as, "We should not violate people's privacy," may match an ethics of principle.

> Value judgments that claim we should produce some result, such as, "We should increase security," may match an ethics of consequence.

Once you have selected an ethical approach for each of the arguments, you can begin with that approach to expand the arguments by asking the questions presented on the corresponding Worksheet, either #4-1, #4-2, #4-3, or #4-4. Then, use the other Worksheets to apply the other two approaches to each argument and perhaps the case itself to see how each argument is supported. The strongest argument will have support from all three approaches, because, as we have shown, it takes all three to cover all five elements of human conduct.

Once you have applied all three approaches, you can then see what you have learned from the process. There may be some agreements that you can use as a basis for working together on the issues (Worksheet #4-5). There may also remain some disagreements. If so, you can develop modified proposals that show respect for the strengths of each view (Worksheet #4-6).

WORKSHEET #4-1

Applying an Ethics of Purpose

Apply this approach by beginning with the agents.

Who are the agents and what should they accomplish (their external purpose)?

_____

_____

What should they become (their internal purpose)?

_____

_____

Which proposals (means) will enable them to achieve these purposes (ends)?

_____

_____

When applying this approach, remember:

- *The purpose or end should be defined not by the proposal, but by the nature, function, or potential of the agent.*

- *You must include both external and internal purposes. The purposes need to cover both what the agent should accomplish and what she or he should become. For example, an individual's external purpose may be to realize a special talent and her internal purpose may be to act with integrity. A firm may have the external purpose of producing products and the internal purpose of developing a work community of mutual respect.*

- *The internal purpose of organizations refers to what kind of community they should become. It looks at the type of human relationships an organization should strive to develop.*

- *Remember the distinction between descriptive and normative thinking. Purpose is used here as a normative term; it states what an agent should do and become.*

WORKSHEET #4-2

Applying an Ethics of Principle

Apply this approach by beginning with the proposal.

What are the implicit principles of the proposals?

_____

_____

Can we will that these principles become universal rules that apply in all such cases?

_____

_____

Do the proposals respect the moral agency of others?

_____

_____

When applying this approach, remember:

- *This approach requires that you construct an implicit principle from the proposal and then see whether you can will that the principle become a universal moral law.*

- *Sometimes you can discover the implicit principle by using the syllogism. The implicit principle would be the major premise.*

- *The principle's universality is based on consistency, not consensus.*

- *The principle is a normative statement, usually formulated as a "should" statement.*

- *If the principle is concerned with distributive justice or with human rights, you will want to use the instructions, and Worksheet #4-3 on the next two pages to explore different types of justice and rights.*

How to Evaluate Implicit Principles that Express Various Notions of Justice and Rights

Ask three questions: (1) What is being distributed? (2) How should this good or these goods be distributed? and (3) What rights follow from this type of distribution?

1. **"What is being distributed?"** asks about the goods or things that some people receive for some reason. The "goods" may range from money to recognition to pain.

2. **"How should it be distributed?"** selects the type of justice that seems to "fit" with the good being distributed. For example, public education could be distributed by membership, while awards could be distributed by contribution. The following criteria for justice include most of the ways we distribute things:

Need	People who need more receive more.
Membership	All members receive equally.
Contribution	People who give more receive more.
Merit	People with special talents or status receive more.
Choice	People get what they choose.

3. **"What rights follow from this type of distribution?"** enables us to discover the rights people have when things are distributed justly. These rights might include:

Human rights	Claims to goods that should be distributed to everyone, such as the right to subsistence.
Civic rights	Claims to goods that should be distributed to all citizens, such as the right to vote.
Contractual rights	Claims to goods that we have agreed to distribute in a specific way, such as wages or benefits.

"What is just?" or "What rights should be acknowledged?" are controversial questions. Their answers lie mainly in our assumptions about the meaning of things (goods). Discussions about these assumptions can sometimes resolve the controversy.

WORKSHEET #4-3

Analyzing Types of Justice and Rights

Using the chart below, list the significant goods distributed in your case. Then select the appropriate type of justice for each good. Most goods should be distributed according to need, membership, contribution, merit, or choice. Finally, select what individual right—human, civic, or contractual—corresponds to the type of justice you have chosen. In some cases, you may find it easier to first assign the individual right and then select the type of justice that belongs to it.

Goods Distributed	Types of Justice	Individual Rights

If you are unsure about how specific goods should be distributed, you can list them below and examine different assumptions about their meaning today. See if some assumptions are more consistent and universal than others.

_____

_____

_____

_____

WORKSHEET #4-4

Applying an Ethics of Consequence

Apply this approach by beginning with a list of all those affected by the decision.

What individuals, groups, and environments will be seriously affected by the decision on the issue?

_____

_____

What will be the positive and negative consequences of the proposals for them?

_____

_____

Which proposal will bring about the greatest overall good?

_____

When applying this approach, remember:

- *Although we often examine the personal costs and benefits of our actions, this approach invites us to consider all groups affected.*

- *Omitting a relevant group will undermine the strength of your conclusion.*

- *Sometimes you will need to balance short-term and long-term consequences or to include future generations.*

- *Since this approach always faces the difficulty of measuring and comparing very different consequences, it is best to include all of the groups involved in developing the measurements.*

If all three approaches support a proposal or facilitate a new proposal, then your argument may be very sound. If only some of the approaches support your argument, then you may want to develop other purposes, principles, and consequences, and at the same time, to experiment with other options, since the strongest argument will have the support of all three approaches.

THE ETHICAL APPROACHES AND THE RESOURCES FOR MAKING DECISIONS

As we said earlier, one or another of the three ethical approaches can be aligned with the value judgments of the different arguments. Each ethical approach also has its implicit observations and assumptions, which you may have discovered when applying them to your arguments. You can use the chart below to compare the ethical approach's observations and assumptions with those you developed from the proposals that brought about the disagreement.

	Observation (O)	Value Judgment (VJ)	Assumption (A)
Purpose	The nature, function, or potential of the agent	The good purposes that the agent should strive to achieve	The agent's good purposes provide the criteria for evaluating acts.
Principle	Implicit maxim or principle of a proposal	Universal, consistent moral laws and respect for a person's moral agency	Persons achieve dignity through willing consistent moral principles.
Consequence	Probable positive and negative consequences	Greatest overall good for all affected	People can measure the consequences for different groups.

ETHICS OF PURPOSE: *We should test the safety of our products, because that will ensure quality products (O), and producing quality products should be one of our purposes (VJ) as a business (A).*
ETHICS OF PRINCIPLE: *We should test our products' safety, because doing so implies the general principle that people should exercise due care toward others (O), a principle that can be willed as a universal law (VJ) by moral agents (A).*
ETHICS OF CONSEQUENCE: *We should test the safety of our products, because this proposal produces more positive and fewer negative consequences than other proposals (O), and we should do what has the best overall consequences for all involved (VJ), assuming our projections are correct (A).*

WORKSHEET #4-5

Working with Agreements

After applying the three ethical approaches to different arguments, you may find some observations, values, and assumptions that are important to all participants. In other words, you may discover some agreements as you have explored the reasons for your disagreements. In the space below, state the important agreements you have discovered.

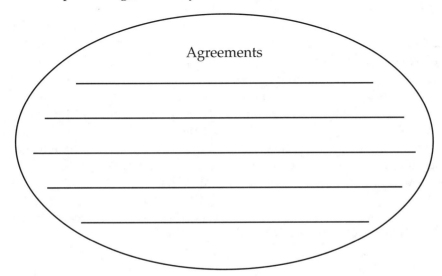

These agreements may serve:

1. As a basis for envisioning new proposals that include the most important value judgments, assumptions, or both.

2. As leverage to negotiate a compromise.

3. As acknowledgment of a common ground.

If possible, write a new proposal that relies on these agreements. If not possible, then use the strengths of each other's views to develop modified proposals.

THE MODIFIED PROPOSAL

Once the resources of different observations, values, and assumptions have been acknowledged and evaluated by applying the three ethical approaches, the next step involves developing a proposal that uses the best resources available. Sometimes the participants will agree on a proposal that emerges from the process. Other times the participants will continue to disagree. When disagreement continues, the participants can usually modify their proposals by allowing the strengths of alternative views to set some limits or boundaries on them.

Suppose you belong to a group of managers who are considering whether to grant a wage increase. You argue for a wage increase because of increased living costs and you think that employees have a right to a salary that covers their living costs (ethics of principle). The alternative view argues against the increase because of decreasing income, and they believe that the negative consequences outweigh the positive (ethics of consequence). If you take a step back from this argument, you can see that both sides have some merit. Instead of arguing for a wage increase at all costs, the alternative view can help you see the limits of your proposal, which would allow you to modify it as follows:

> "The company should increase wages *unless* the increase thrusts it into financial difficulties."

Or you could also say:

> "The company should increase wages *if* the increase does not harm the company's prospects for profitability."

These limits do not mean that an increase is impossible. Perhaps low wages are causing poor morale, lower productivity, and therefore lower profits. So an increase in wages may even increase prospects for profitability. Employing such limits means that the participants have learned from one another. In most cases, the best proposal shows an awareness of its limitations.

Use Worksheet #4-6 to list the strengths of each view, which may be their observations, value judgments, or assumptions, and then use these strengths to modify your initial proposal.

WORKSHEET #4-6

Developing the Modified Proposal

**Strengths of
Your View**

_____

_____

_____

_____

_____

**Strengths of
Alternative View**

_____

_____

_____

_____

Modified Proposal

We should _____

_____

unless/if _____

_____

Q & A SESSION III

Q.   I have some questions about the chart relating the three ethical approaches and the elements of arguments on page 60. Can you really observe the "nature, function, or potential of an agent"?

A.   Suppose a group at a medical center considers whether to train its employees in the Ethical Process. From an ethics of purpose approach, it would begin by thinking about its identity. What kind of place is it? People could probably agree that it is a health center staffed by people with different types of training and abilities. This answer would be an "observation." They could also observe how it currently fits in with other health services and the general health care system. Such an analysis would describe what we could call "the nature, function, or potential of an agent."

Q.   OK. How do you get from this descriptive statement of an organization's function to a norm for decision making?

A.   Basically, you get there by relying on assumptions. Some people may assume that the purpose of health centers should be limited to promoting physical health, while others may assume that health centers should have a broader purpose, even including the promotion of spiritual health. The "good" purpose really arises out of the discussion between observations and assumptions. The key assumption behind this approach, however, is that the medical center does have a "good" purpose that it should strive to achieve. If training in the ethical process helps to achieve it, then it would be justified.

Q.   Can an ethics of principle help here?

A.   The ethics of principle approach doesn't begin with a vision; it begins with an intention to do what is right.

Q.   And what does one observe in this approach?

A.   This approach does not directly take into account the particularities of a situation. It does "look at" the implicit principle of any proposal, so this could be called an observation. It is the only descriptive aspect of this approach.

Q. But it is stretching it a bit to call that an observation.

A. Somewhat. Still, it makes sense to speak of "observing" different levels of abstraction, which is what this approach requires. All of our observations, of course, are made from some perspective, or if you will, rely on some assumption. So when we "look at" the proposal and "see" an implicit principle, what we see will depend on our assumptions.

Q. How would you tackle the question of training from an ethics of principle approach?

A. First I would "observe" the implicit principle, or maybe I should say that first I would construct it and then "see" if it really fits the proposal. What about this: "People should receive the training they need to do their jobs." That "looks" like a possible implicit principle. Can we will that it become a universal moral rule? I think so. It affirms that there should be some congruence or consistency between skills and job requirements. Not to provide training but to demand good decisions would be inconsistent or contradictory. You could not will that as a universal moral law.

Q. I get it. The third approach, an ethics of consequence, seems the easiest.

A. It may look easier because this approach appears to rely more on observations than the other two. As you begin comparing different possible consequences, however, it can become overwhelming, especially when people disagree about the meaning or value of different consequences. In such cases, the other two approaches can complement an ethics of consequence.

Q. You see all three working together?

A. Yes. If they support different proposals, then there is usually more work to do. They can also correct one another and generate more material for each approach to consider. Sometimes three heads are better than one.

EXAMPLES OF USING
THE THREE ETHICAL APPROACHES

To show how to apply the three ethical approaches, we will apply them to two issues we have already raised: health care (p. 18) and personal development versus group loyalty (p. 41). We will examine the questions that the ethical approaches elicit and point out some of the areas they open for reflection.

Ethical Analysis of Universal Health Coverage

Before we begin applying the three ethical approaches, we need to ask whether the argument for universal health care (on p. 18) already expresses one or more of the different approaches. Look at the value judgment: "When we are able to provide care for some, we should provide it for all." This does seem to fit with an ethics of principle, and a type of justice. We can also examine the assumptions. The first assumption ("We are all part of an interdependent health care system.") probably relies on an ethics of purpose—the purpose of a health care system. The second assumption ("Health care is a necessary condition for self-fulfillment.") may also rely on an ethics of purpose—the end of human existence as self-fulfillment. Or it may rely on an ethics of principle—the right to those conditions necessary for self-fulfillment as a human right for all moral agents. We can also notice that the argument does not appear to address consequences. By applying the three ethical approaches, we can expand the tacit uses of an ethics of purpose and principle and add to the dialogue an ethics of consequence.

Ethics of Purpose.   An ethics of purpose begins with identifying the agent, which in this case would be the government. Or, we could say that in a democracy the government is not the decision maker; the people are. So, what is our purpose in having a government? This question can elicit a much larger discussion that we cannot entertain here. For now, let's take one side of this political controversy and say that the purpose of government is to protect people's rights. Given that purpose, we can ask, "Does universal health coverage protect people's rights?" One could argue, on one hand, that the lack of coverage today, especially for children, prevents people from developing their potential, and this could be interpreted as a denial of their individual rights. On the other hand, taxing some citizens so all can have health care may be seen as infringing on other rights.

These reflections seem to pull us into an analysis of assumptions, but we will turn instead to exploring the question of the agent's internal purpose. Let's ask, "What kind of society should we become? A society where everyone has opportunities for self-development? A society where everyone feels included? A democratic society? Does universal health coverage promote or detract from achieving this society?" Let me ask it this way: "Can we reach the ideal of a democratic society without universal health coverage?"

Ethics of Principle.　An ethics of principle begins by stating the implicit principle or maxim in the proposal. Let's begin with the argument's value judgment, since it could work as the implicit principle or maxim for the proposal: "When we are able to provide care for some, we should provide it for all." Can you will that this should become a universal moral law? We probably need to define what we mean by "care," or by "health care." If we reword the sentence to read, "If we can prevent someone from suffering, then we should do it," then we could probably will that this principle become a universal moral law. Remember, we are trying to be consistent, not to establish consensus. Let's turn to the second aspect of an ethics of principle. Does this proposal respect others as moral agents? You could say that it is too paternalistic. But you could also argue that it does respect moral agency because it creates the conditions necessary for people to exercise their moral agency.

Under an ethics of principle, we could also ask about the fairness of universal health coverage, and whether people have a right to such coverage. How should we distribute health care? Is it a commodity that should be distributed by contribution? Should it be distributed by need? What is fair, not only for the people who need health care, but also for the people who pay for it? Are there some principles of justice that we can apply here?

Ethics of Consequence.　What difference will universal health care make? What groups will be affected? How should we categorize them? Universal health care coverage will certainly have a different effect on some than on others. For the wealthy, the effect will likely be more taxes. For many of the poor, or working poor, it will be more accessible care. For the middle class, it will probably mean different coverage, but without much reduction in costs. You might discover a better way to develop the groups. We could think of the consequences for different stakeholders, such as the different medical professionals, the insurance industry, and the recipients of care. Then we would have a different set of consequences to compare and contrast. This can easily become an overwhelming task, because the change to universal coverage would have so many different effects.

One possible path through this complexity is to take a more systemic approach. We could look at how the current health care system works. Then we could analyze how to change the system so that it would have fewer negative consequences and more positive consequences. What we should strive to achieve is a proposal that fits our national purposes, is consistent and fair, and has the fewest possible negative consequences.

Ethical Analysis of Joan's Choice

When we look for the implied ethical theories in this case (p. 41), we see that the one side relies on an ethics of principle ("People should keep their promises.") and the other on an ethics of purpose ("People should increase their competence and develop their potential."). This second value judgment, of course, could also function as a principle. Furthermore, in the assumptions, both sides look at consequences, and so all three ethical approaches are touched on. By applying the complete ethical models, we should be able to increase our resources for evaluating the relative merits of these different statements.

Ethics of Purpose.   The two agents most directly involved are Joan and her team. Joan's external purpose is like that of every other human being: to develop her potential. This may be further defined for Joan as developing her competency in her work. Her internal purpose is to become a mature person with integrity. How do we know about Joan's purposes? We know she is a human being and as such she has the general purposes of human life. If we disagree about human purposes, or about whether they even exist, then we would need to examine our assumptions about human existence. But whether we agree or disagree, we can still look at what could be justified with the purposes we have proposed. Does staying hinder or promote Joan's development?

What do we find when we focus on the team? If the team is an agent, it means that it can make decisions, and in fact, it has, deciding that Joan should stay. Is the team right? The team's external purpose is to produce some product or provide some service. Its internal purpose is to develop the kind of working relationships that are appropriate for people working together. On one hand, if Joan stays when she really wants to go, I can imagine that the team will not achieve its internal purpose, even though it may achieve its external purpose. On the other hand, the team may feel justified in keeping people to their promises, because a team that does not honor promises may not develop the same type of working relationships that it could if promises were kept.

Ethics of Principle.   An ethics of principle can examine the value judgments presented by each side and see if they can be willed as universal moral principles. It seems that the value judgments of both sides can. Also, all the value judgments seem to respect others as moral agents. So what do we do with this conflict of principles? In this specific case, can we give more weight to one than another? Could we say, "People should keep their promises unless it blocks their development"? I doubt it. Maybe, however, the "promise" to work together was a type of promise that never implied one would forgo career advancement to keep it. Are promises at work different from promises in other situations? This line of inquiry may lead us to explore our assumptions about work relationships to see whether they differ from other types of relationships.

Ethics of Consequence.   The consequences that concern us here are those that affect Joan and the team. What are the likely consequences if she stays? If she leaves? How can we measure them? One method is to assign the various consequences positive and negative values. Let's try it using a scale ranging from a negative five to a positive five:

Joan stays.		Joan leaves.	
Teamwork is not interrupted.	+2	Joan's life plan is furthered.	+4
Promise keeping is supported.	+3	Promises are broken.	−3
Joan's career is hindered.	−3	Joan contributes elsewhere.	+3
Team cohesiveness is damaged.	−2	Team must adjust to change.	−2
Totals	0		+2

If this assignment of values is correct, it seems Joan should leave. Would the other two approaches support a similar decision? An ethics of purpose might, if it led us to emphasize the purpose of individual self-fulfillment. An ethics of principle would lead us to consider whether the right to individual freedom should override the duty of keeping promises. Or is freedom finally dependent on people's keeping their promises?

Connecting an ethics of principle with an ethics of consequence could prompt us to ask if breaking promises has any consequences. If so, then we should return to our list of consequences and add one about breaking promises. As we continue to explore the relationships among the three ethical approaches, we may find a number of ways they can correct and enhance one another.

The two issues we have examined—the first more social and the second more individual—could have been dealt with differently. Other questions could have been pursued, and they might have generated more important questions. How much one needs to explore different approaches depends on the kinds of disagreements among the people involved. Just as with the argumentative model, so it is with the ethical approaches: The task is to locate and understand the differences among alternative positions, and then to use the differences to learn more about each of them.

CHAPTER FIVE

The Ethical Process as an Argumentative Dialogue

When you combine the descriptive work outlined in Chapter Three, which brings forth implicit and taken-for-granted resources, and the normative work presented in Chapter Four, which provides different criteria to evaluate arguments, you have a complete model for dealing with controversial issues. Whether you can use this model in dealing with current controversies depends on whether the participants will choose to engage in dialogue. Throughout this workbook, we have stressed the importance of good reasons and of good relationships. Although sometimes dialogue may not be warranted, in most situations, the possibility of dialogue exists if participants will take the risk of creating it. The "Storyboard" on the next page expresses some of the aspirations that provide the context for combining good reasons and good relationships to form what we call "argumentative dialogues."

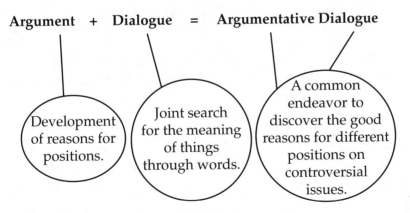

Argument + Dialogue = Argumentative Dialogue

Development of reasons for positions.

Joint search for the meaning of things through words.

A common endeavor to discover the good reasons for different positions on controversial issues.

For most people, argument and dialogue do not belong together. Putting them together here reminds us that we are using argument as a method of inquiry as well as advocacy, and that we are working together to find the best decision possible.

A STORYBOARD
FOR
ARGUMENTATIVE DIALOGUES

The Setting

An issue becomes controversial because people have different opinions about the right course of action and they must decide what to do.

Because they have different opinions, the participants also bring different resources to the table. They gain access to these resources through exploring the reasons for their disagreements. Instead of being discouraged by a scarcity of resources, they are encouraged by the potential abundance of resources for making the best decision possible.

Acknowledging their differences provides them with an opportunity for the mutual development of their resources.

The Actors

Participants recognize one another and their organization as **moral agents**. Moral agents have the ability to recognize options, to choose one option over others, and to give reasons for the choice. In other words, people are seen as free and as rational.

The communality of participation overrides any separateness caused by hierarchy. Rank and power are not used to intimidate others, which increases the likelihood that the group's decisions will stand up to outside scrutiny. Through dialogue, participants expand their thinking beyond their previous stances and become involved in a **learning community**.

Action

Participants **engage in a common inquiry**, discussing the reasons for different positions. They look for resources in all positions presented, seeking those that will enable them to make the best possible decision.

They **participate in the creativity of dialogue**, as they elicit from one another the implicit meanings of what they have said and begin to discern what should be said.

The "tools" for the argumentative process are questions. The participants begin by asking questions, "Why?" "So What?" and "How Come?" They carry the dialogue forward by asking **questions of inquiry** that seek to uncover the implicit resources that lie behind the participants' positions. Once they have reached an understanding of one another's view, they apply different ethical criteria to evaluate their strengths. The process moves back and forth between advocacy and inquiry.

When they have reached an agreement, or have run out of time without reaching one, they **decide what should be done**.

Argumentative dialogues do not happen all at once; they entail a continual **process** peppered with the pauses and interruptions you would expect when people must make a decision. Even after a decision is made, the dialogue usually continues in response to changing conditions and new challenges.

Purpose

People become engaged in the Ethical Process because they are faced with controversies. One purpose of argumentative dialogue is **to make the best decision possible** given the available resources.

Another purpose is to **develop a moral community**. As participants examine different values and assumptions, and imagine the effects of their decisions on others, they also increase their awareness of the common human struggle for meaning and justice.

MAPPING ARGUMENTATIVE DIALOGUES

In a pure dialogical process, the participants become involved in a synergistic process wherein they discover what to say. Such dialogue cannot be planned. Participants need to wait, listen, and then give voice to what they have never thought before.

Argumentative dialogues are less pure and not so open-ended. They are a response to a specific question: "What should we do?" They seek an answer.

The "map" that follows can serve as a guide for an argumentative dialogue. It combines the descriptive work of uncovering the values and assumptions of different views and the normative work of evaluating these arguments with different ethical approaches. The steps are numbered to remind participants to first develop each other's arguments so they can use them to uncover assumptions. Steps 1 through 9 parallel the Worksheets in Chapter Three. Use them to develop the material for these steps. Before you fill in box #10, the normative evaluation, review the worksheets on applying the three ethical approaches to issues in Chapter Four. This map assumes that each side will be able to develop modified proposals by incorporating the strengths of the other view into their own. The different sides could also, of course, develop a new proposal, agree on one modified proposal, or continue to disagree.

The map can be used:

- to develop class presentations on controversial issues, showing how partners can work together to develop resources for better decisions.

- to write papers that explore the strengths and weaknesses of alternative views.

- to outline the key arguments of essays and articles, showing both the explicit and implicit aspects of the argument.

**Remember, a map is not the same
as the territory it represents.
This map should be used as a guide
for thinking, not as a substitute!**

A MAP FOR ARGUMENTATIVE DIALOGUES

QUESTION

1
What should we do about _____
_____

PROPOSALS

2
We should _____
_____
_____

5
We should _____
_____
_____

Why?   **OBSERVATIONS**   Why?

3
Because _____
_____
_____

6
Because _____
_____
_____

So What?   **VALUE JUDGMENTS**   So What?

4
I believe we should _____
_____
_____

7
I believe we should _____
_____
_____

How Come?   **ASSUMPTIONS**   How Come?

9
I assume that _____
_____
_____

8
I assume that _____
_____
_____

10
NORMATIVE EVALUATION: What can be supported by

an ethics of purpose? _____
an ethics of principle? _____
an ethics of consequence? _____

MODIFIED PROPOSALS

11
So, we should do it unless (or if) ___
_____
_____

12
So, we should do it unless (or if) ___
_____
_____

CONCLUSION

Remember the old joke about the man searching for something under a streetlight late at night? Someone came by and asked what he was doing. He answered that he was looking for his house keys. The passerby asked where he had lost them. He replied he had lost them on the other side of the street. "So why not look there?" "Because," the man said, "the light is better over here."

We don't always find the resources for making good decisions on the path of least resistance. Often they become available to us through acknowledging our differences and our disagreements.

The Ethical Process of decision making is a communicative practice. Its success depends on our capacity to respect our differences and our willingness to mutually explore our different "worlds."

Engaging in dialogue with those you disagree with does not require that you lack conviction about important matters. It does require, however, that you not be so mired in a position that it becomes impossible to listen to the reasons of those who disagree with you.

The Ethical Process, which is motivated by the moral commitment to a more humane and just world, requires that people have convictions. At the same time, as people become involved in the hard work of ethical reflection, they may find themselves participating in the development of moral communities and discover their convictions strengthened in the process.

Although the Ethical Process has been outlined in orderly steps in this workbook, it is much more perplexing in everyday life. There all the elements we have sorted out are jumbled together. Still, in many situations, awareness of the process can help us to look in the right place for the resources to make good decisions.

How to Use the Syllogism to Uncover Implicit Value Judgments

An important part of the Ethical Process is the development of controversial arguments, that is, arguments that support different proposals about how to respond to controversial issues. In the development of these arguments, it is fairly easy to formulate proposals and observations that support them. It is not so easy to figure out the value judgment on which the proposal and observation rely. In many situations, this value judgment remains implicit. To uncover it, we can use the logic of the deductive syllogism.

Deductive syllogisms are argumentative structures that contain two premises or reasons and a conclusion. The structure of these elements is such that if the premises are true, the conclusion necessarily follows. Here is a standard deductive syllogism:

> *Humans are mortal.*
> *Socrates is human.*
> *Therefore, Socrates is mortal.*

For a deductive syllogism to be valid, it must comply with several conditions or rules. By valid, we mean that the conclusion necessarily follows from the premises, that the logic of the argument is correct. One of the most important rules is that deductive arguments can have three and only three terms. The terms are called the minor term, the major term, and the middle term. The subject term of the conclusion is the minor term, and the predicate term of the conclusion is the major term, and the term that is in both premises, but not in the conclusion, is the middle term. So the terms in the Socrates argument look like this:

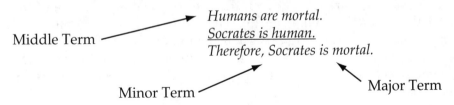

Middle Term

Humans are mortal.
Socrates is human.
Therefore, Socrates is mortal.

Minor Term   Major Term

As you can see, the major term is located not only in the conclusion but also in the first premise. Thus, the first premise is called the major premise. And the second premise is called the minor premise because the minor term is located there as well as in the conclusion. The middle term is located in both premises, but not in the conclusion. We can make this clear by using symbols for the different terms and circling the middle term.

Humans are mortal.	Ⓗare M
Socrates is human.	S is Ⓗ
Therefore, Socrates is mortal.	S is M

How can this information help us to find the implicit value judgment of a controversial argument? It can help because controversial arguments use the same logic as the deductive syllogism. This may not be immediately apparent, because controversial arguments begin with proposals rather than with reasons or premises. If, however, we reverse the order of the three sentences of a controversial argument, we see that they parallel the three propositions of the deductive syllogism. Consider the following arguments:

(1) Logic of Controversial Argument	(2) Order Reversed	(3) Logic of Traditional Syllogism	(4) Symbolic Form of Syllogism
Proposal Observation Value Judgment	Value Judgment Observation Proposal	Major Premise Minor Premise Conclusion	Q are P S is Q S is P

In the first column (1), which is the form of a controversial argument, we begin with the proposal and follow with an observation and then a value judgment. In the second column (2), we have reversed the order. This allows us to see the parallels between the controversial argument and the logic of the deductive syllogism (3). The value judgment parallels the major premise, the observation parallels the minor premise, and the proposal parallels the conclusion. The third column can then be rewritten with symbols (4) to make clear the position of the deductive syllogism's three terms.

Because of the parallels between a controversial argument and the deductive syllogism, we can use the rule of three and only three terms to figure out an implicit value judgment. Once we have written the complete argument, we can use other rules of validity to evaluate an argument's logical strength. Let's see how this works by starting with the following proposal and observation.

Proposal: *Everyone should be rewarded,*
Observation: *because everyone contributed.*

How many terms have been expressed so far in the proposal and observation? There are three: "Everyone," "rewarded," and "contributed." So we know that the value judgment, which is already implicit here, will not introduce another term but can be constructed from the terms already expressed. Since the term "everyone" has already been used twice, and the other two only once, it makes sense to use the other two terms in the value judgment in a sentence like "Whoever contributed should be rewarded." We then have the following argument:

Proposal: *Everyone should be rewarded,*
Observation: *because everyone contributed.*
Value Judgment: *Whoever contributed should be rewarded.*

Once we have developed the value judgment, we need to know whether it is the correct one, that is, whether this particular value judgment fits with this proposal and observation. We can find out by applying another rule for valid deductive syllogisms: the rule of the distributed middle term. To understand how this rule works, we will rewrite the controversial argument we just developed as a standard deductive syllogism. (In terms of the four columns on the previous page, this is a move from column 1 to columns 2 and 3.)

Whoever contributed should be rewarded.   Major premise
Everyone contributed.   Minor premise
Everyone should be rewarded.   Conclusion

Now we want to see if the middle term has been distributed. What does it mean for a term to be distributed? It means that we have said something about all members of the class that this term names. For example, in the first argument about Socrates, the middle term is "humans" (H) and in the major premise, we say, "All humans are mortal" (H are M). In other words, we say that "all" of the class of "humans" has been distributed into the class "mortal." So the syllogism is valid.

Is that also true of the middle term in our argument about who should be rewarded? What is the middle term? Remember, it is the term in both premises but not in the conclusion: "contributed." If we look at the major premise, it says in effect that all who contributed will be distributed into the class of rewarded. So the argument is valid.

Let's apply the rule of the distributed middle term to another argument, to determine how it may help us see its strength. We'll begin with a proposal and an observation and then use the syllogism to develop the implicit value judgment:

Proposal:	*We should test employees for drugs,*
Observation:	*because drug testing will improve safety.*

What is the implicit value judgment? We first look for the middle term. It is "safety." So we know that the value judgment will contain the term safety. Safety is something we value, so we can write a value judgment as follows:

Value Judgment:	*We should promote safety in the workplace.*

Is our argument valid? We can find out by asking if the middle term is distributed in at least one of the premises. Let's rewrite the argument as a deductive syllogism.

Major Premise:	*We should promote safety in the workplace.*
Minor Premise:	*Drug testing will improve safety.*
Conclusion:	*We should test employees for drugs.*

For "safety" to be distributed in one of the premises, we would have to say something about all of the class that it names. Neither premise does that. Furthermore, the major premise does not repeat the major term of the conclusion—"testing employees for drugs." Nor does the minor premise repeat the minor term of the conclusion. So the syllogism is not valid. By not valid, we mean that agreement with the premises does not lead necessarily to agreement with the conclusion. The argument "might" be true, but it is not "necessarily so." Yet, the argument seems to have some persuasive force. Is this force sound? To find out, let's try to rewrite the syllogism, but this time we will deliberately follow the rule of distributing the middle term. Here is how we can make it look like the valid syllogism about Socrates that we examined earlier.

H are M	*Safety is an organization's obligation.*
<u>S is H</u>	<u>*Drug testing improves safety.*</u>
S is M	*Drug testing is an organization's obligation.*

Now the major term—"organization's obligation"—is in the major premise. The minor term—"drug testing"—is in the minor premise, and the middle term—"safety"—is in both premises. Furthermore, the middle term is distributed in the major premise, all of safety is distributed to "organization's obligation." So this formulation appears valid.

You may wonder if some sleight of hand is going on in the rewrite. Let's go back to the first formulation and think about why it is not valid. The argument stated that since we should have a safe workplace, we should do drug testing. The weakness of this argument is that there may be ways to have a safe workplace other than by drug testing. Perhaps one could do other kinds of tests, such as a computerized hand-eye coordination test, to insure safety. In other words, because safety is not distributed, the premises do not prove that the conclusion necessarily follows from them. Now when we rewrite the argument, we make it valid, but we are still left with the question whether drug testing is the only way to create a safe workplace, or whether there are other ways to achieve the same result.

Another way to distribute the middle term, besides saying something about all of the term's class, is to negate the term's class. In other words, you can distribute through exclusion. If you exclude all members of a class from another class, then you have distributed them. Look at the following argument, first as a controversial argument and then as a deductive syllogism:

We should not do drug testing.	*We should respect the right to privacy.*
Drug testing does not respect privacy.	<u>*Drug testing does not respect privacy.*</u>
We should respect the right to privacy.	*Therefore we should not do drug testing.*

The middle term is "right to privacy," and in the minor premise or observation, it is distributed through negation. The premise says in effect that none of the class "right to privacy" can be distributed to the class of drug testing, or in other words, the "right to privacy" is excluded from "drug testing." So the syllogism passes the test of distributing the middle term. Another rule for a valid deductive syllogism concerning a negative premise and conclusion is that if there is a negative term in one premise, then the conclusion must also be negative, which is the case here. So this argument appears to be valid. Since negative premises can distribute through exclusion, sometimes you may want to rewrite a controversial argument with a negative conclusion and premise, to see if you can strengthen the logic of the argument.

The use of the syllogism, then, can help us in several ways to discover the implicit value judgments on which we rely when we take positions on controversial issues and begin to develop support for them. The rule of three terms shows us that once we have developed the proposal and the observation, we have probably already developed all the terms we need to formulate the implicit value judgment. Second, we know that the middle term in the observation—the term not in the proposal, but in the observation—will also be in the value judgment. Finally, we can be fairly certain that if we can rewrite the argument so that the middle term is distributed in at least one of the premises, our argument has validity.

APPENDIX TWO

An Argumentative Dialogue on Drug Testing

Max   We need to decide whether we should begin a drug testing program in our organization.

Sara   Yes, and I've been thinking about this. I don't think we should.

Max   Why do you say that?

Sara   I think drug testing invades a person's privacy.

Max   How does it do that?

Sara   Well, the employer gains information about a person's private life.

Max   I agree with that. But so what?

Sara   I believe we all have privacy rights.

Max   I agree with you there, too, but we need to consider other factors than privacy. I think we should do drug testing, because it will decrease drug-influenced accidents.

Sara   I suppose it will, but I don't know how widespread drug use is.

Max   I don't know for sure either, but it seems certain that if we do not institute a drug testing program, we will have some accidents.

Sara   Well, I think we need more information before we can agree on the extent of drug use in our organization. Even if drug testing increases safety, that doesn't mean we should do it.

Max   Can't we agree that we have a responsibility to maintain a safe workplace?

Sara   I think we all want a safe workplace.

Max   So you agree with my argument that we should have drug testing because it will increase safety and we should maintain a safe workplace.

Sara   Your observation might be true and I do value safety, but I don't agree with your proposal. You seem to agree with my reasons too.

Max   Yes, I value a person's privacy, but sometimes we have to give a little to gain a lot.

Sara   That's true, but who gives and who gains? Look, our observations and value judgments are different, but they do not contradict each other. How come we still disagree? I think it is because we have different assumptions. I guess that if I assumed that employers could do whatever they wanted with their employees, then I would agree with you.

Max   Well, I don't know if I assume that.

Sara   I certainly don't. I don't think anyone should have that kind of power over other people.

Max   So, what do you assume about the power that employers should have over employees?

Sara   What comes to mind for me is the common law notion of "master-servant." You know, the employer is the master and the employee is the servant. I find this notion feudalistic. It doesn't fit in a democratic society like ours. I assume that people do not give up their rights when they enter the workplace. You seem to assume that employers have a right to act like masters of their servants.

Max   Well, I wouldn't put it that way. I do assume that employers have a responsibility for safety. Isn't that how its always been?

Sara   Well, what has been doesn't tell us what should be. Anyway, I find your assumption intriguing. Let me ask you, "Who should be most concerned about my safety?"

Max   You should be.

Sara   Right. Doesn't it seem that employees would have a greater concern for a safe workplace than employers? After all, it is their safety we are talking about.

Max   Yes, but to agree with you, I would have to assume that workers will actually do what is best for them, and that what is good for employees is good for the organization. With our present work force that is a risky assumption.

Sara   Perhaps, but we are dealing with assumptions here. Remember McGregor's distinction between Theory X and Theory Y styles of management. Theory X assumes that workers want to avoid work and responsibility. Theory Y assumes that workers want to be productive and responsible. Your assumption seems more like Theory X.

Max   Perhaps we do have different approaches here. I hadn't connected management theory to the drug testing issue before. I think of myself as using a Theory Y management style, but in this case, I am not sure I trust workers to avoid drugs.

Sara   That may be one source of our disagreement.

Max   Perhaps. I am certainly not ready to disapprove of all drug testing. Although I appreciate a person's right to privacy, it seems that we talk too much about rights and not enough about responsibility. If I think about what I would have to assume to agree with you, it seems I have to assume that individuals who claim their rights will also be responsible.

Sara   I assume so.

Max   Well, that seems too individualistic to me. We need to consider an organization's culture and how groups influence individual behavior. Drug testing sends a message about what kind of organization we want to become. A lot of people follow the crowd. They are not the responsible individuals you imagine.

Sara   I agree that we are shaped by our society and certainly we see a rise in drug use, so I guess more people have followed the trend.

Max   Perhaps you cannot have responsible individuals until you have a responsible society.

Sara   Or is it the other way around?

Max   It must be some balance of the two. Drug testing could change the social trend of drug use.

Sara   Yes, and it could also decrease individual responsibility by violating individual rights.

Max   Since we are talking about the probable impact of a drug testing program, we might gain some clarity by applying an ethics of consequence.

Sara   Your arguments seem to align themselves with that approach.

Max   The primary groups impacted by our decision will be the workers, the people we serve, and the organization. When I look at the consequences of drug testing on these groups, the positive results outweigh the negative.

Sara   How do you figure that?

Max   The positive consequence will include lower risk of accidents for the workers, better service, and therefore more success for the organization. A negative consequence might be that some individuals would feel we have violated their rights. At the same time, they may appreciate a safer workplace, which would be another positive consequence.

Sara   You also need to consider the long-term consequences of drug testing upon employee morale and trust. We could also include the workers' families in our analysis. What will be the effect on them when they learn that their family members have to be tested for drugs? Perhaps in the long run, the overall consequences will be negative.

Max   I see that our decision affects more groups than I first thought, but I still favor drug testing.

Sara   Perhaps our decision should be guided by an ethics of principle.

Max   Your argument seems closer to that approach.

Sara   Respecting people's privacy can be willed as a universal moral law, and it does treat people as moral agents.

Max   I wonder if drug testing has an implied principle that could become a moral law.

Sara   A proposal that allows one group of people to test another group seems to set up an inequality that would be hard to universalize. If the implicit principle was that everyone should be tested for fitness, I suppose it could be universalized. This proposal, however, must also treat people with respect to fully align itself with the principle approach.

Max   Whether our decision respects others may depend more on its implementation than the decision itself.

Sara   Perhaps. Let's think about this from an ethics of purpose approach.

Max   The purpose of the organization is to provide quality services. To do this we need a reliable work force. So drug testing could be seen as a means toward achieving the organization's end. The end justifies the means.

Sara   We need to consider not only what the organization should do but also what it should become. I mean, we need to consider the kind of workplace we should become.

Max   Well, it should be a place where people work cooperatively together in getting the job done.

Sara   Yes, so the question is whether drug testing will promote such cooperation. If cooperation requires trust, then drug testing would not, because it signals a lack of trust between the organization and its work force.

Max   It seems that the internal and external goals conflict.

Sara   Right. It seems that the three ethical approaches favor not testing. The analysis of consequences has not provided a clear-cut answer. The ethics of principle seems to favor not testing because of the requirement to treat others with respect, and the ethics of purpose certainly gives as much weight to not testing as to testing. What do you think?

Max   I agree that our decision should respect persons and should not diminish the quality of our work community.

Sara   I do agree with you that our decision should insure a safe workplace. Perhaps drug testing would have some positive consequences that I had not previously considered.

Max   We need to find a balance between influencing group behavior and encouraging individual responsibility.

Sara   Let me suggest a modified proposal: "We refrain from drug testing because of its infringement on individual rights until and unless we observe an increase in accidents and poor productivity."

Max   Well, your modification does include my basic concern. I appreciate that. What about modifying my proposal? "We should perform drug testing, unless we discover that it causes a decrease in individual self-esteem and individual responsibility."

Sara   Your qualification does state what might be some of the consequences of violating people's privacy, but I don't think that our decision should be based solely on probable consequences. We also need to include what we learned from an ethics of principle and purpose. In any case, I think we should find out more information about employee attitudes toward drug testing. Since we are doing something to them, we need to listen to them first.

Max   We are supposed to decide this ourselves. Maybe that is the crux of the disagreement between us.

Sara   It is more complicated than that. We need to value safety and privacy, and we need to balance honoring individual responsibility and influencing collective behavior.

Max   Where such a balance exists may only become apparent when we begin to implement our decision.

Sara   Could be. I think I now understand the strengths of your position, but I have also gained confidence in mine.

Max   OK. Let's postpone the implementation of drug testing for six months. During that time we will monitor safety, and we will begin conversations with employees about their participation in insuring a safe workplace.

Sara   I agree with that. If we discover an increase in accidents or poor services that is due to drug use, we will begin a testing program.

Max   I think we should share this with our co-workers.

Sara   Yes. The department should go through this process too.

Max   Thanks.

Sara   And thank you.